# More Sales Less Marketing

**How to take the yuck out of selling**

Frances Pratt

First published 2024 by Frances Pratt

Produced by Independent Ink
independentink.com.au

Copyright © Frances Pratt 2024

The moral right of the author to be identified as the author of this work has been asserted.

All rights reserved. Except as permitted under the *Australian Copyright Act 1968*, no part of this publication may be reproduced, stored in a retrieval system, or transmitted in any form or by any means, electronic, mechanical, photocopying, recording or otherwise, without prior written permission from the publisher. All enquiries should be made to the author.

Cover design by Catucci Design
Edited by Anna Von Zinner
Internal design by Independent Ink
Typeset by Post Pre-press Group, Brisbane

ISBN 978-1-7637688-0-2 (paperback)
ISBN 978-1-7637688-1-9 (epub)
ISBN 978-1-7637688-2-6 (kindle)

**DISCLAIMER**

Any information in the book is purely the opinion of the author based on personal experience and should not be taken as business or legal advice. All material is provided for educational purposes only. We recommend to always seek the advice of a qualified professional before making any decision regarding personal and business needs.

This book is dedicated to my kids.
Their imagination, cuddles and love are my world.
I fully acknowledge their mastery and shared insights
on negotiations and selling.

# Contents

Introduction ... 1

## Section One
## Your Relationship With Sales ... 5

Chapter 1   I Hate Selling! ... 7
Chapter 2   What's Wrong With Marketing? ... 21
Chapter 3   You Are the Sales Champion ... 32
Chapter 4   What Are You Really Selling? ... 50
Chapter 5   Let Trust Guide Your Sales ... 63

## Section Two
## Taking a Client View of Your Business ... 81

Chapter 6   Shut the Back Door! ... 83
Chapter 7   Focus on Your Client ... 92
Chapter 8   Sales is a Numbers Game ... 101

## Section Three
## Take It to the Streets — 127

| Chapter 9 | Clients Will Listen When You Speak to Them | 131 |
| Chapter 10 | Meetings That Rock Your Client's World (And Yours) | 151 |
| Chapter 11 | Are You Really Listening? | 168 |
| Chapter 12 | Meetings, Questions and Finding a Fit | 184 |
| Chapter 13 | Proposals Are About Your Client – Not You! | 205 |
| Chapter 14 | Reframing Your Results for Great Selling | 217 |
| Chapter 15 | Asking Doesn't Need to Feel Yuck! | 231 |
| Chapter 16 | You Never Stop Selling | 251 |

*Conclusion* — 267
*Acknowledgements* — 271
*About the Author* — 273
*References* — 275

# Introduction

> "If we walk far enough," says Dorothy, "we shall sometime come to someplace."
>
> — L. FRANK BAUM, *THE WONDERFUL WIZARD OF OZ*

Thank you for choosing this book. You won't regret it.

In this book we will walk together and come to someplace that helps you be better in sales and business.

This book is for all of you who squirm when you think of being salesy. Sales doesn't have to be like that. Read on, and let me show you.

I hope you all love the movie *The Wizard of Oz* as much as I love it. Many years ago, I started using the characters and storyline to help explain selling in a new way. Even if you don't like or love it, I am sure you will understand the use of archetypes and stories to support your new love of selling.

This book is in three sections.
1. Exploring your relationship with sales and how to change it
2. Helping you understand the key elements of **Great Selling**. How to think, feel and do **Great Selling**.
3. Taking it to the streets and walking with your client on your sales journey.

**Section One** is about you and your relationship with sales. By reading these chapters, you will better understand why so many people hate selling and how to change that. We will examine what **Great Selling** is and why learning more about it is imperative for you and your business. This section gives you the critical foundations of **Great Selling** that we will use as we move through the book's other sections.

We all fear things in life and business. Just like Dorothy, I will take you into a brand-new world – in Technicolor! You will meet new characters, and better yet, you will learn new things about yourself. You will discover that you can sell and had it inside you the whole time.

**Section Two** is about getting to know your business from your client's perspective. We explore why businesspeople often forget the customer and how to build in a client focus so you don't ever forget again. This section also starts to flesh out some reasons people fail in business and selling and what to do about it.

One of the things I love about business is the different characters you meet along your path. Some are kind, and some are not. Some think they are a pussy cat, brainless and heartless. Sometimes, they are, and most often they aren't. The gold lies in your client, partner, and colleague relationships. This section helps you to explore these.

**Section Three** encourages you to take these ideas and skills to the streets and learn more about your clients, how they buy, and what and how they are interested in buying from you. It walks you through each step in the **Great Selling** process and shows you how to do this in a way that makes you feel comfortable and successful.

**Great Selling** is about knowing and sharing your Yellow Brick Road. It starts with understanding what your client wants and what they are willing to do to solve their problem. Your job in selling isn't to push them down that road — it's simply to introduce the concept and encourage them to start.

So, dear reader, put on your Ruby Slippers and come with me.

Let's dig in.

# Your Relationship With Sales

**Section One**

Love it or hate it (and I am tipping that if you have picked up this book, you are in the second category), the truth is that ALL businesses sell to stay alive. Selling is one of the oldest professions known to humankind.

There is nothing wrong with selling, and here's the truth: Once you understand this, you will find that owning this role in your business is liberating. More than that, following the Yellow Brick Road outlined in this book will allow you to grow and prosper without feeling like you are selling your soul.

So, I encourage you to read on. Embrace your feelings and work with me through this book.

Let me take you to the movie *The Wizard of Oz* when Dorothy first lands in Oz. She is frightened. Everything has turned from Black and White to Technicolor. The only familiar things are Toto and her house. To add to this, she has killed someone, and there is the murmur of people she can't see twittering around her.

Glinda, the Good Witch of the North, comes floating down in a magnificent frock in her bubble. Her first job is to get Dorothy off her porch. She doesn't need to answer every question just to get Dorothy to take her first step.

Let me be your Glinda. Come off the porch and let me show you the Yellow Brick Road to the Emerald City of "loving selling".

CHAPTER 1

# I Hate Selling!

"People lose a lot of time in hating others, and there's no fun in it at all."

— L FRANK BAUM

## Now, What to Do About That?

This chapter (and book) is for business owners who cringe at the very idea of selling; because of that, they don't sell!

I am sure you have heard the advertisements on the radio stating proudly, "We don't have salespeople!" This always makes me laugh. Then I think to myself, "How are you in business?"

Every business started by selling something to someone. The business owner overcame their fear, talked to people, and asked them to buy. When I write it like this, it sounds so easy – right? But I know you picked up this book because you don't feel this way. You don't want to push people. You fear they will think you are selfish, demanding, pushy and "salesy" if you ask.

Selling, or being seen as salesy, is one of the greatest fears for new and highly accomplished businesspeople. And yet — they overcome this fear. Why? Their desire to "change the world," be of service, and offer value helps them overcome it. But here's something I know — the businesspeople who don't overcome this fear fail.

## You Can Learn to LOVE Selling.

I have spoken with so many people who hate selling, and I have been able to turn them around to loving it. That's a bold statement, I know. But I have seen it time and time again. Connecting what you do with why people want to buy from you opens up a whole kaleidoscope of new options and adventures. It offers freedom to both your clients and you.

Your job now is to trust me. Suspend that doubt, do the work and reap the rewards.

## Why People Hate to Sell.

I have learned three things from working with and helping people reframe their distrust of selling:

1. People hate to sell because they think it is about manipulating people into buying something from

them – something that they don't need or can't afford and don't want. In their minds, they conjure up a picture of the dodgiest, slimiest salesperson in the world and then try everything in their power over their words, actions and intentions for people NOT to think of them that way.
2. People hate to sell because they don't like the idea of someone saying no or asking questions that might interfere with their perception of the value they deliver to their customers.
3. People hate to sell because they focus on themselves (the seller) and not their client (the buyer).

The truth is that people are often so scared of what others might think of them that they might see them as pushy or salesy. This stops them from even trying because the idea is so irksome. These thoughts prevent them from selling the right way and often create exactly the experience they are trying to avoid.

Where do these ideas come from? The truth is that there is **Great Selling** and **Bad Selling**.

I am sure you have had the experience of walking into a shop and feeling like you are being targeted. You feel that the salesperson in the shop is ONLY interested in what's in your wallet and how much you have to spend. Equally, there are times when you walk into a shop and feel totally out of place like you are not welcome because the salesperson in that shop shows you exactly what they are thinking – that they are disinterested and think you are a waste of their time. Both of these are examples of **Bad Selling**.

## Let's Understand Bad Selling.

What is **Bad Selling**?

### 1. They talk at you.
Bad sellers start by talking. They talk at you. They try to push you down a particular path before understanding you and your needs.

### 2. They make it about them.
They make it about what they want and not what you need. They need the sale or the money. They show you that in their words and actions.

### 3. They focus on the quickest path to what they want.
They don't give you time to ask questions, explore or discover. They use all the tactics and ploys to achieve their end as quickly as possible.

### 4. They handle objections.
Objections are obstacles to what they want. Objections are the enemy of the sale. They treat them with disdain and with the disrespect they think they deserve.

## I Call Bad Selling "Crocodiles and Dinosaurs".

**Bad Selling** has been around forever. It has had successes, but these are diminishing. It is an attitude and methodology that has had its day. In short, bad sellers are dinosaurs! Yes, this way of selling still exists! But (and it's a big but) their time is over.

When I hear people talk about this, I remind them about crocodiles and dinosaurs.

"Yes, there are crocodiles, and just because there are crocodiles still on Earth, that doesn't mean we are in the age of the dinosaurs."

The truth is that **Bad Selling** is dying. It is dying because it is no longer effective. Because it doesn't represent who and what we are as consumers. And it isn't what businesses and business owners want to be a part of.

Today's consumers are more intelligent, better researched, and savvier. They see through the shim sham and vote with their feet and wallets.

I am sure you have experienced **Bad Selling**, but you don't have to choose to be like this to succeed. I encourage you not to. Business success comes from embracing **Great Selling**.

This book will convince you there is such a thing as **Great Selling**. It is accessible and possible for you to implement, and you can start today.

## The Three Keys to Great Selling

There are three areas to work on when you approach **Great Selling**:

1. **Mindset** – thinking like a great salesperson and eliminating the flim-flam, dodgy image in your mind.

2. **Activity** – once you have your mind "right", it's time to take actions that follow and reinforce this mindset.
3. **Results** – lastly, we must reframe how you view your sales results.

Getting the desired results from actions aligning with your values creates a virtuous cycle. When you get this virtuous cycle working for you, you will see the true power of **Great Selling**, and it will feel less yucky! You will enjoy (or even love) selling.

I have had countless people tell me just that.

> "I would never have thought that I would actually say that 'I Love Selling!'"

So, let's take this journey together, and I will release you and your business.

## It Starts in the MIND.

**This step is imperative!** If you approach your client when you are not in the right frame of mind, you will waste your time, frustrate yourself and reconfirm the idea that you can't do selling. You will reinforce the crocodile of **Bad Selling** and falter before you start.

We will cover this in more detail in Chapter 3 with some exercises and ideas to explore. But here are the three key steps.

 **Mindset – Think Like a Salesperson.**

**Know what you think.**

Be honest with yourself about how you feel about sales and selling. Once we have that out on the table, we can change it.

**Choose to think differently about sales.**

**Great Selling** is *NOT* pushy, interruptive, manipulative, or painful.

**Great Selling** is helping someone who has a problem fix that problem or fulfil a need. It's that simple. Stop thinking about it as selling and start thinking about it as **helping people buy**.

The key to thinking like a salesperson is to focus on your client and not make it about you.

 **Activity – Focus on Doing the Right Things.**

Okay, you have your head in the right space. Now, let's get out there and use your new attitude for good!

**Get organised.**

Make time to go out and talk to current and prospective clients about what you do. Have daily, weekly, and monthly targets for staying in contact with people by picking up the phone or seeing them. (More on this in Chapter 8.)

**Be open and transparent about your sales process.**

You are there to guide your client, so build a Client Roadmap – a step-by-step guide to how you engage with them. (More on this in Chapter 7.)

**Follow up.**

Have a strategy for following up with your clients. An easy way to do this is to ensure you have set the next step with your client. (More on this in Chapter 12.)

### Step Three: Results and Rewards.

You have the right mindset and are doing the work. Well done! Now, keep going. One great way to help you **focus** is to have clarity on what you are trying to achieve and to **reward** yourself for taking steps towards that.

**Know what you want to achieve.**

Set goals! How many new clients do you want to sign up, and in what timeframe? What extra income does your business need? Make it **CRUNCHY**! (More on this in Chapter 8.)

**Break down your goals.**

Set and **track** monthly and weekly goals so you can see and reward progress. Make yourself accountable. Put a big poster on the wall with your targets and your achievements. Make it public!

**Reward yourself!**

Each new client meeting you attend, the new proposal you get out there, and the phone calls you make get you closer to your goal. Celebrate! Whatever your poison is —hot chocolate or champagne. Be sure to let people know by doing a happy dance (or whatever your preferred method is).

•●•

## Great Selling is Helping People Buy.

When I am working with teams, I often ask them to tell me about a great sales experience they have had. And very often, they can't. The reason is that when you are the recipient of a great sales experience, it feels like someone has helped you to buy something you need or want by helping you understand how it can help you. Right there is the essence of **Great Selling**. It isn't pushy or self-orientated. It focuses on helping the other person solve a problem or fulfil a need. It focuses on them and their buying process, helping them make a good buying decision, irrespective of the outcome.

## Great Selling Has a Process.

As we run through this process, I want you to keep this front and centre in your mind.

Great Selling is
**HELPING PEOPLE BUY.**

It's about them and not about you. It's about helping them fix a problem or fulfil a need. When you get this first piece of the puzzle right, the rest of the process follows logically. It feels better, and it is better.

### Step One — Listening.

If you are going to help someone, you first need to know what they do and don't want. Sometimes, this is an easy process; sometimes, you must glean it from their actions and reactions.

Listening involves all your senses and is isolated from the rest of the sales process. I mean that until you are sure you understand the person, you can't move on to the next step.

People buy something because they have a problem or a need. You are there to help them uncover and understand that need – that's listening. (More on this in Chapter 11.)

## Step Two: Find a Fit.

Where are you? They have a problem, and you have a potential solution to that problem.

Now the question is – does it fit? Walk with your client through the fit to their budget, timeframe, and other needs. Fitting things together is about explaining how your solution meets their needs and solves their problem. The best way to demonstrate this is to use stories of people you have helped. What was their problem, how did you help them, and what was the result?

There will never be one story that encapsulates your clients' needs and motivations, so it is important to explore different solutions until you are sure you are on the right track.

Sometimes, there isn't a fit. When this happens, be honest and say so. You can still be helpful by helping your client find someone else who might work out for them.

How do you know you are on the right track? Well, that involves more listening! Listen with your eyes and brain to see and interpret facial expressions and body language. (More on this in Chapter 14.)

## Step Three: Look for Objections.

Yes! Look for objections. They are there waiting; the sooner you get your client to bring them out, the sooner you can answer them.

If there are common objections that I think will be relevant to this client, I often try to bring this up first.

> *"I have worked with several clients that have a similar business, and initially, they were worried about _____. Once we had been through the solution and they had spoken to some of our clients, they were happy that this wouldn't happen with our solution."*

Once you have uncovered and answered one objection, it creates trust and allows for more discussions and objections. (More on this in Chapter 14.)

## Step Four: Create Value.

You know when a sales relationship works well because you create value for all parties. At a minimum, this is you, the client, and your business. However, this may well encompass the community and other stakeholders.

A **Great Sale** is one where everyone wins.

1. If you take this view that you are always looking to create value, then the other precursor steps make perfect sense.
2. In Australia, it is estimated that 20% of new small businesses will fail in their first year, and up to 60% of start-up businesses fail within five years of launching. These numbers come from the ASBFEO (Australian Small Business and Family Ombudsman)[1].

3. Failure in business can be avoided if we just get out there and embrace our clients and help them to understand all the value that we have to offer them. But in order to do this, you first have to understand the value, not from your perspective, but theirs.

•●•

I know that I have put a lot into this first chapter. And there is a reason for that. I want you to keep going. The rest of the book is about helping you break down all these new ideas and put things into action.

You can do this, and I can help you, but only if you keep reading.

But more than that. You have to do the work. Mindsets don't change from reading a book. They change because the ideas spark a light. We follow the light, and we try new things. We try these new things on for size and see how they feel. We make mistakes and have new experiences, which help to remodel how our brain works and educate us to make better choices.

I can change the way you think, feel and do selling, but only if you come on the journey with me.

I have already mentioned *The Wizard of Oz*. It is one of my favourite stories. If you have ever heard me speak, I am sure you will have heard me talk about it.

So, for the duration of this book, you are Dorothy.

But there would be no story if Dorothy chose to stay in fear and not get off her porch. If she had decided not to explore and stayed with Toto, she wouldn't have discovered anything new about herself. She wouldn't have had the adventures, discovered her strength, and found her way home.

I ask you to take my hand and get off the porch. Let me introduce you to the Yellow Brick Road of **Great Selling**. I know you will thank me.

CHAPTER 2

# What's Wrong With Marketing?

> "I think you are a very bad man," said Dorothy. "Oh, no, my dear; I'm really a very good man, but I'm a very bad Wizard, I must admit."
>
> THE WONDERFUL WIZARD OF OZ BY L. FRANK BAUM

## Marketing Is Essential.

I think the very first thing that I must tell you is that **I LOVE marketing**. It is a great discipline that is essential to building an awesome business. You know there must be a but. So, here it is.

Most business owners rely too heavily on marketing and have forgotten the key step of selling and connecting personally with their clients.

Like the 'Wizard' trying to be a wizard, marketing has gone rogue! It has been touted as a universal panacea for all business ills. Want more clients? Just market more. Cash flow problems? Try marketing. It's not your fault, but you are involved. Those touting marketing have been successful because they play on some of your deepest fears – your fear of selling and being seen as salesy.

The only way to put the marketing monster back in its box is to confront this fear. I remember when I was a kid in my bed at night, knowing snakes were writhing on the floor, only to find that they magically disappeared when I turned the light on.

Big people are not so different from little people; we just learn to hide our fears and insecurities better. We learn to push these fears deeper; sometimes, we are so good at this that we forget they are there.

I encourage you to name your fears, put them on the table, turn the light on, and let's explore them together. Let's put the crocodile back in the zoo where it belongs.

## Marketing and Selling Are Sisters.

One of the key problems with marketing is that it seems to have lost its connection with selling. Marketing and selling are sisters. They go together. They complement one another. Selling without marketing is beating your drum and getting a few people to dance but missing the noise and joy of a big, fun party. Marketing without selling is thinking everyone will be coming to your party, but they either don't show, or you are not ready to ask them to dance.

It's time to get the family back together. It's time to reunite the sisters and watch how the sympatico between them works to augment your business and bring you more clients. Better than that, get you clients that genuinely match you and your business. It feels like magic when this happens – but it's just good business.

## Why Am I Worried About the Marketing Problem?

The problem I see is that businesses spend too much time (and money) on marketing when they don't really understand what motivates their clients to buy from them. They market what they want to sell or think they are selling. They have worked so hard to make this product or service that they want to sell and get it out there!

How do I know this? I have been working with business owners for a long time. I talk to people in business every day. When people are starting, I listen to what they say. Here are some samples:

- Once I get my website done
- I am doing a brochure
- I must finish my proposal (or insert another marketing thing here).

Wrong. Wrong. Wrong. It makes me want to cry.

It's putting the cart before the horse and then wondering why you go nowhere.

Yes, you need marketing materials in both digital and analogue formats. But, and it's a massive **BUT**. You **HAVE TO KNOW** what your clients **want** to hear **first**. When you know this, you will know what they will respond to and what they want to say yes to.

Marketing materials only make sense and have value when they speak to your clients. It is not about what YOU have done but what THEY need, want, and desire. And often, these things are at odds with each other. What you think you are selling and why they buy can be very different. This knowledge is the golden ticket to your success. It **is** the Yellow Brick Road.

If you stop reading here or remember nothing else – remember this:

## YOU ARE NOT YOUR CLIENT.

You don't have to believe me. Here are ideas from some of the greatest thinkers in management over the last 50 years.

Peter Drucker, known as the "Father of Modern Management", wrote extensively about the importance of understanding clients. He is famous for this quote: "The purpose of business is to create and keep a customer."

From the Father of Modern Management to the Father of Modern Marketing, Philip Kotler was emphatic about businesses tuning into their clients' desires and needs.

And lastly, one of my favourite thinkers and authors, Seth Godin, says: "Don't find customers for your products, find products for your customers."

I bet you're thinking, "Who is she to tell me this? How does she know?"

## Let Me Share My Story About Making This Exact Mistake.

In 2011, I was pregnant with my first baby. I had only recently started my own business, and I was convinced I had to put an online "Sales for Normal People" program on the internet so people could learn from me while I was growing a baby.

I wrote the program, launched a website, blogged, recorded the videos, and wrote the workbooks. Everyone told me it would be excellent and that my material was great and so needed.

I was convinced that all I needed to do was to launch the program. I had spent a lot of money. I had to birth this idea to save the world.

I launched my program the week my baby was born. And how many sales did I make in the first six months? None. A BIG FAT ZERO.

I learnt this lesson the hard way. I am a great seller but NOT good at marketing. I was too concerned about what I wanted to say and what I was doing. I didn't stop to talk to my potential customers about how they want to buy and consume.

I started exploring why once I got my brain back together (post-baby). I spoke to people and went to my brain's trust at *HerBusiness*. Their response? Do some Client Avatar Interviews. Talk to the people who are in your target market. Simple!

The following week, I did seven interviews. They were wonderful and enlightening, and I even sold a couple of my programs.

But the biggest a-ha moment came through in every single interview. My target client was convinced they couldn't sell and could do nothing about their fear. It was too deep, too dark, too much a part of them. They wouldn't sit there, watch the videos, and do the work. They didn't think it would work. They needed someone to coax them, guide them and be their coach. They needed me.

Based on these insights, I changed what I was doing. I changed what I was saying to speak to their fears. I gave them me, either one-on-one or in a small group setting. The sales started.

And the irony is, if I hadn't done that work, the work I now ask you to do, I wouldn't be able to sit here and write this for you – showing you that **Great Selling** involves humility and service.

**Great Selling** is a product of letting go of your preconceived ideas and getting in touch with the people you dream of helping so you CAN help them. In doing so, you help yourself, release your expertise and feel the wonder of helping others and changing people's lives.

I know I am gushing a bit there, but it's true. It is my story. I have helped people birth businesses that are thriving.

## Why Does This Matter in Great Selling?

Talking about yourself and what you are selling is a part of being the crocodile of "bad" selling. Taking that same message to the mass market is simply a waste of your time and money. Clients want to hear about themselves, not you. That's when people tune in. Clients don't want to hear about what you are selling; they want to know three things:

1. That you "see" them and deeply understand their pain.
2. You have a solution that might be able to help them, so they want to learn more about you and your solution.
3. You have a process that makes sense to them and shows them the big-picture steps to a better result or solution to their problem.

When you don't deeply understand the value proposition from the client's perspective, you are literally wasting your time and money. Your marketing is ineffective because it doesn't "speak" to anyone, let alone your clients and what they want and need. You are screaming into the void, hoping that anyone might hear you and respond. It's not going to happen.

Some of my best friends are marketers, and after they finish choking at the title of this book, they agree with the premise.

The premise is this:

> Your first job in business is to
> get to know your best clients deeply.

You don't have to believe me. Some of the greatest business minds of our time agree with me.

> "The aim of marketing is to know and understand the customer so well the product or service fits them and sells itself."
>
> — PETER DRUCKER

The problem with some modern marketing is that for the last ten years, small to medium businesses have been told that if they "market" well, they won't have to sell. Some marketing companies have sold the idea that you will win business if you get enough visitors to your website or Facebook page or clicks on a lead magnet.

This just isn't true.

Great marketing is great. But the truth is that great marketing is based on deep client insights. And, as businesses grow their ability to sell diminishes because they build walls to keep themselves away from their clients. The insights diminish, and so do the sales.

You can't do sales or marketing. You must do both.

The problem has been created because business owners hate selling. This has been played on. Putting the cart before the horse is easy when you are told what you want to hear. The cart that promises clients but can't move because the horse is on the wrong end. But there comes a time when the Emperor realises he has been sold something that doesn't exist. In the face of reality, he sees that he is wearing no clothes, and there is nowhere to hide.

This book is about putting the horse back in the front of the cart. It's about the steps we must take to reacquaint ourselves with our most loved clients. To understand their motives and what they value deeply and then deliver that.

## Sales Is an Imperative at All Stages of Business.

If you are just starting, your time and money are finite resources. You know the reality of having to face the client every day. Relish this time and use it to collect data and information on how your clients feel and react. Immerse yourself in this gold, which will pay dividends as your business grows. Listen and learn and feel your way.

As our business grows, it gets easier to think, "We've got this". We don't need to sell anymore. We know our clients and how they think and feel. Well, maybe you do, and maybe you don't. Clients change and grow, too. And more than that, they forget what value you are delivering if you are not there to remind them. Selling never stops. (More on this in Chapter 16.)

Maybe you hate selling, and maybe you don't.

Maybe you love marketing, and maybe you don't.

Either way, one thing we can (hopefully) all agree on is that business is about customers. Clients seeing, buying, consuming and getting what they bargained for and much more.

This book is for business owners who love their clients. It is for the entrepreneurial thinkers. It is for those who want to know, give more, and yearn to keep ahead of the wave.

Most of all, this book is for doers and those in business who want to know more about their clients and their business. They don't just want to know more; they want to put things in place and take the actions that improve their business for their people and clients. This book will help you take action.

I must be honest. Sales really does get a bad rap. In the last ten years, I have turned people from hating to loving selling. Let me share with you what I have learned.

## Why People Don't Talk to Their Clients.

I am about to talk about what you should do. But before I do that, I must explain why people don't talk to their clients.

I know there are some of you reading this that think, "Of course, you must talk to your clients".

But after working with businesses, here are the top eight reasons you forget to talk to your clients:

1. You think we don't have anything to say.
2. You aren't sure who the "right" person to approach is.
3. You think that you might be annoying or bugging them.

4. You are scared they will think you are trying to "sell" them something.
5. You are shy.
6. You think you should know this and don't want to ask dumb questions.
7. You don't want to be criticised or discover something you don't want to hear.
8. You have a new product or service but are unsure if it fits your market or who will like it.

I have heard all of these things from businesspeople, just like you. You may relate to one or more or none of these. But here is the real question.

When did you last walk a mile in your client's shoes?

When was the last time you understood from your client's perspective exactly what value they receive from their interactions with you, your business and your product and service?

Getting to deeply understand what motivates your clients and what they value about you, your products, services, and your business should always be the number one thing you do in business.

I am asking you to join me in reopening the Sales Door, not the crocodile trap, but the door marked **Great Selling**. Keep reading because next, I will challenge you to take it personally and work with me so you can move into a sales rhythm that delivers you clients that love to say yes to you and that you love to work with.

I am asking you to be your own Sales Champion.

CHAPTER 3

# You Are the Sales Champion

"You've always had the power, my dear. You just had to learn it yourself." Glinda the Good Witch.

— L. FRANK BAUM, *THE WONDERFUL WIZARD OF OZ*

## Take Ownership of Your Role to Connect With Your Client.

You are the sales champion – you just don't know it yet.

I'll tell you something that's no big secret. Not everyone loves selling. I know it can feel like a hard but necessary slog on your journey of starting and building your business.

What if I told you it didn't have to be that way? With my help, you could learn how to sell in a way that works for you. You could grow to understand the science and art of selling so you can more easily bring in clients and increase profits in your business.

What if I told you that you could grow to LOVE selling? It's bold, I know and totally possible. I know this because I have walked this journey with people just like you and helped them achieve exactly this.

There are many secrets to selling. I will share my favourite **11 Secrets of Sales Champions** in this chapter. These will help you become more comfortable, confident, and exceptional at selling.

Sales is like no other discipline in business. It must be learned when facing your client. There are things I can teach you and show you. But the only way you can understand and do selling is to **do it**. Selling is all about taking action and learning on the job.

I have put this chapter at the start of the book to encourage you to start practising today. Start talking to people, and explore and uncover your sales style. It is there – you just need to get out and talk to people, explore with them, learn more about yourself and them. You can place each gem you find and learn into your crown of sales.

At the end of the chapter is a link to a perfect cheat sheet to print for your wall so you can remember to implement and practice these secrets daily.

 **Intention is Everything!**

Before you do anything, before you pick up the phone, write an email, or pat the dog good morning, you need to think about where your head is at.

> Start the day with the intention that you will sail through your sales tasks and get the answers to your questions. You are going to learn more about you and your client today.

Make a firm decision to choose your attitude for the day. Permit yourself to deal with whatever the day throws at you with clarity and grace.

**Be clear** about what you are trying to do, what value you offer to your clients, and why you started your business in the first place. You had intent – a reason to start your business. Now is the time to take that intention to fruition.

**Be honest** with yourself and with others about what you can do and how you can help them (or not). You will win only through building trust with your clients and prospective clients. Honesty means saying yes and no in equal measure.

**Find the win:win** in all situations. Winning at sales feels good for you and everyone in the game. It's about honouring you, your staff, your clients and showing them the possibilities. It is about giving your clients the information they need and allowing them the space to decide.

## Secret Two: Have a Plan.

As the late, great Stephen Covey said, "Start with the end in mind." Another way to say this is:

> "If you don't know where you're going, any road will take you there."
>
> — LEWIS CARROLL

Set goals for yourself in your sales role. Every great salesperson sets (and often exceeds) big, hearty targets they make for themselves. The very act of setting a goal helps to set your intention and puts you on the right track.

As one of my first managers told me, "Don't expect what you don't inspect". So, whatever your goals are, set up a way of recording, tracking and reporting on them.

This step is vitally important because you will do the things you measure.

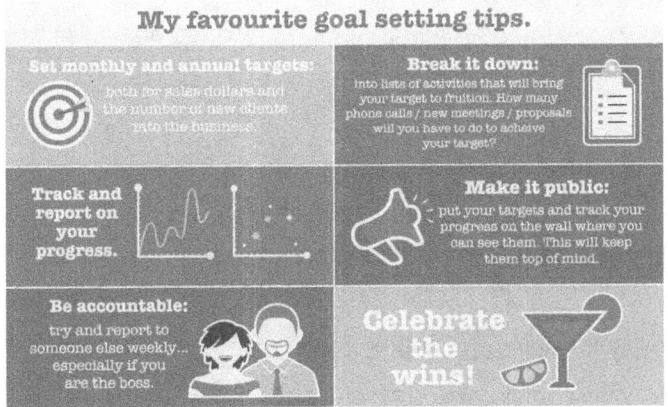

**My favourite goal setting tips.**

**Set monthly and annual targets:** both for sales dollars and the number of new clients into the business.

**Break it down:** into lists of activities that will bring your target to fruition. How many phone calls / new meetings / proposals will you have to do to achieve your target?

**Track and report on your progress.**

**Make it public:** put your targets and track your progress on the wall where you can see them. This will keep them top of mind.

**Be accountable:** try and report to someone else weekly... especially if you are the boss.

**Celebrate the wins!**

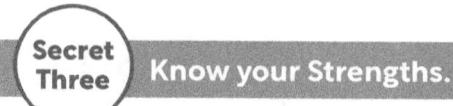

## Secret Three: Know your Strengths.

Great businesses, like great relationships, are built on flexibility around a core idea and an exchange of value. The key here is to know your core strengths – the foundations of your business and the base DNA that holds you and your business together. These are probably related to why you got into business in the first place.

**Your strengths will help you win over your clients.**

Show them how your strengths add value to their business. And don't forget to "get crunchy" – find out where and how you add value and what that means to them.

**Your strengths are qualitative and quantitative.**

Where they are quantitative, get the figures. It is so much more influential if you can say "I can improve your bottom line by 19%" rather than a vague "blanket statement" about what you deliver to your clients.

Where they are qualitative, collect the stories and case studies to make sharing these with new potential clients easy.

**If you're not sure of your strengths, ask your clients.**

Not sure where to start? Here are three great questions:

1. What value do I deliver to you?
2. Why do you like working with me?

3. What makes me different from other companies that could do this for you?

And while you are asking those questions, why not ask these too:

"If there was one thing I could improve in my business to make it easier for us to work together, what would that be?"

"Do you know anyone else you think would benefit from working with me?"

## Secret Four: Put Your Client Goggles On.

We get so busy in the day-to-day running of our business we forget that we are actually in the business of doing something for someone.

We all know that without clients, we don't have a business. Yet so many business owners think that seeing and understanding what a client wants just once is enough. It's not. Our offerings and their needs change over time. Failing to put on your client goggles regularly is how business models and businesses go bust.

> **When you forget to check in with your clients to see what has changed, you lose touch with how you can help them improve their business and deliver value to their clients.**

The other key here is that over time, our clients forget what it was like before we fixed all their problems. It is part of our job to help them remember all the great things we have done. It's a bit like your Anti-Virus software. To do its job, it doesn't need to show you how many files it has scanned, etc. The software companies do that so that when it comes time to renew the licence, you do.

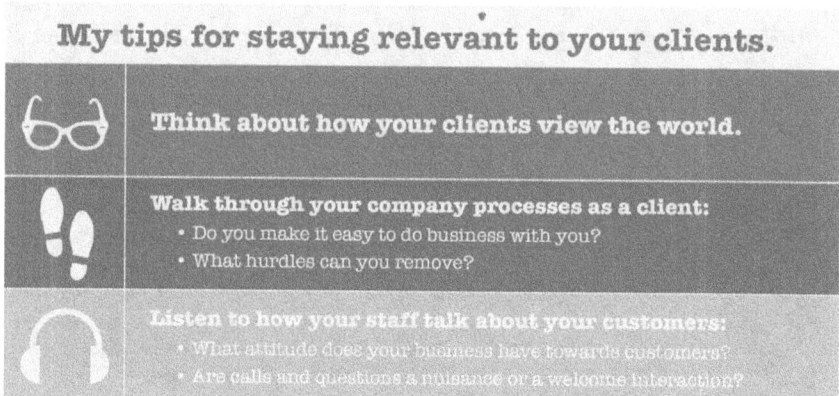

**My tips for staying relevant to your clients.**

- Think about how your clients view the world.
- Walk through your company processes as a client:
  - Do you make it easy to do business with you?
  - What hurdles can you remove?
- Listen to how your staff talk about your customers:
  - What attitude does your business have towards customers?
  - Are calls and questions a nuisance or a welcome interaction?

**Most importantly**, see your clients face-to-face and ask how they experienced your business. How do they think you might improve your service to them?

## Secret Five: Preparation Is Great. Practice Is Better!

Sales and marketing are often grouped together. And for good reason: they are undoubtedly complementary disciplines. However, there is one key area where sales and marketing differ.

**Marketing** is how you seek to understand and effectively deliver your product or services to the market. Marketing "puts the product on the shelf". The Marketing Mindset wants to get everything right **before** you put it in front of a client.

**Selling** is persuading or influencing an *individual client* to buy a product or service from you. It's often referred to as "conversion of the potential". Selling is something you **can only** get right by practising it in front of a live client. The sales mindset says, "Let me take what I have and go and see what clients think of it".

**The sales process focuses on active or engaged prospects, that is, people actively looking for a solution to a problem** they know about. A great sales process and salesperson can convert this potential to reality. They should also help uncover and convert latent prospects (potential clients) from within your target market.

**In sales, nothing replaces face-to-face contact with an actual, live potential client.** Preparing your marketing collateral and having this ready is essential to having the confidence to get out in front of clients. **But** it's during face-to-face encounters that you'll learn firsthand how to determine what and why this client wants to buy. You get to see their steps and how to help them make their buying decision.

These insights are what you put in your marketing, not the other way around.

**So, my advice is: don't wait!**

Now is the time to get in front of your target audience and get firsthand experience in understanding their needs and problems and how they want to buy from you.

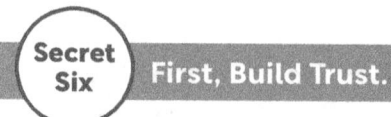

## Secret Six: First, Build Trust.

The simple truth is that before you can help someone to buy, they must trust you. In your client's eyes, building trust starts with you, your business, and then the product or service they want to buy.

**The Foundations of Trust**

You should look to build these foundations of trust with every client interaction.

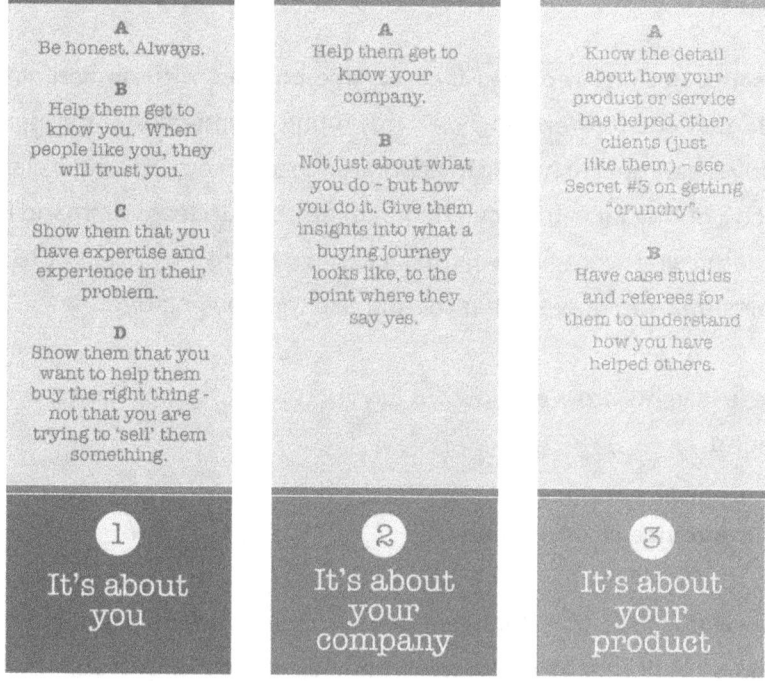

**1. It's about you**
A. Be honest. Always.
B. Help them get to know you. When people like you, they will trust you.
C. Show them that you have expertise and experience in their problem.
D. Show them that you want to help them buy the right thing - not that you are trying to 'sell' them something.

**2. It's about your company**
A. Help them get to know your company.
B. Not just about what you do - but how you do it. Give them insights into what a buying journey looks like, to the point where they say yes.

**3. It's about your product**
A. Know the detail about how your product or service has helped other clients (just like them) - see Secret #5 on getting "crunchy".
B. Have case studies and referees for them to understand how you have helped others.

When you are successful at building trust, it speeds up the buying process. It also means your clients are more likely to continue to be your clients and recommend you to others.

 **Listen!**

Listening is your number one tool in selling. People talk about salespeople having the gift of the gab, and whilst that's often true, this "gift" is only effective when they first listen.

> **Listening means you're concentrating on what the other person is saying.**

When people think about listening, they start with words, which only comprise 7% of communication. The greater majority (55%) is from body language and eye contact, and the remaining 38% comes from vocal inferences such as tone, pitch, and speed.

**You need to use your ears AND your eyes.**

It's clear that you need to use your ears to listen, but you also need to use your eyes to "hear" what your client's body language is saying. All of these inputs need to be interpreted by the brain so that you gain an understanding of their meaning.

Once you have that understanding, the next step is to see if your interpretation is correct, and you can only do that by saying what you believe you've heard and checking with your client to ensure that you have it right.

> **Sales Trap**
>
> **Don't assume** that you are right. **Have a hypothesis**, but make sure that you **check with the person** you are meeting with that you have it right. I **use an introduction** such as:
>
> "From what I have heard today it sounds like your main problem is _____. Is that right?"

My sales rule on listening is captured in this saying:

> "You have two ears and one mouth. So you should listen twice as much as you talk."

 **Be Yourself!**

When teaching non-salespeople how to sell, I find their number one aversion is that they don't want to put on a persona to sell, to become something they aren't. They believe they must be someone else while "doing" sales. This is often borne of the idea that great salespeople must be extroverts.

Let me set you straight.

> The world's greatest salespeople are honest and don't put on a different persona when they sell.

I know some highly successful salespeople who are introverts. The truth is that our clients aren't stupid, and they can see straight through a phoney.

**Great Selling** experiences come from a discussion focussed on what your potential client is trying to achieve and how you can help them achieve that. To do this, you must get intimate with your client (and I don't mean holding their hand).

Intimacy allows you to ask those questions that shed light on the real problem for your client and what type of solution will work within their business context. Each person's version of the problem you solve has nuances that need to be addressed in your solution.

> **Only by being yourself can you exude confidence in what you are doing and saying.**

This confidence helps the client to trust you. When they do, they'll share their problem so you can apply your expertise.

## Secret Nine — Know Your Stories.

Stories are an excellent tool for all salespeople. They are especially important for people who don't like selling because they are easier to use. When you tell a story, you feel more natural and don't feel like boasting. You are telling your clients' stories about how you helped them and how that made you feel. This will naturally exhibit confidence in yourself and how you serve others.

Stories educate and inform. Human beings have been telling stories since time immemorial because they work. They work because they have a beginning, middle and end that educate. Stories are how we learn.

They tell your prospective client about your success:

- In starting and continuing to run your business.
- Helping a client to overcome a problem.

Ideally, the problem should be a problem that your prospective client also has – now they are listening! We love to listen to stories where we see a part of ourselves in the characters.

**Stories are memorable.**

Memorable stories have three key ingredients. They tell the listener what the story is about. They describe the situation, the people and their problems. Lastly, they end with a solution that talks about what you did and how you delivered it.

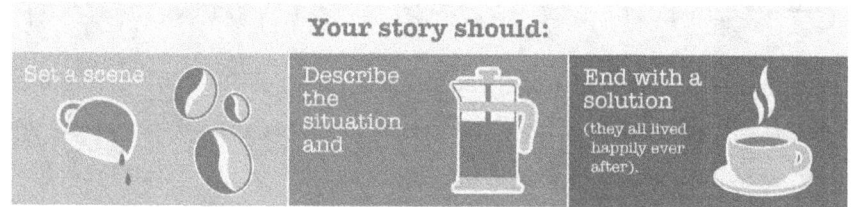

Your stories should emphasise your points of difference (why people have chosen to work with you). Give your listener insights into how you operate and deal with your clients. The more you can show people you know about your prospective client and their problems, the better they can resonate with your story.

> If you do this well, your prospective clients will want to listen because they have the same problem you are describing and can see the steps you took to help other clients overcome it.

 **Secret Ten — Know Your Buyer. Know Your Market.**

**Great Selling** is about helping people buy.

First, you must understand your market and the individual buyer to do this. The more you understand their problem and how they want to buy, the easier it is for you to find them and help them.

**Great salespeople are curious.**

Curiosity is about observing and digging to find the problem and its presentation. You need to ask lots of questions. Be bold!

**What are the biggest problems your clients face?**

Get into your client's head and know what keeps them awake at night. Finding new clients will be a breeze if you can successfully answer this question with a believable answer.

**What are the biggest issues in my industry?**

Consider the key problems people tend to have when dealing with your industry. How do you address these? State how you do this upfront so that people know you are different in how you work.

**How is the problem presenting for this buyer?**

Before you meet them, dig, dig, and dig some more. You can learn much about your buyer from their website, social media, or a Google search. The more you know, the more you can target your pitch and make it visceral for them.

**How does your buyer learn and understand?**

Everyone absorbs information differently. When you meet with your client, look for signs of how they process information and then adjust your approach to suit. If I am speaking with a softly spoken and detail-oriented person, I slow and quieten my normal speech and look for ways to give them detailed information, such as spreadsheets and case studies. This person will typically want all the facts and figures before committing to a decision. If you're not sure – ask them. Most people are happy to tell you.

**Is there a buying team?**

Often, in a business, there is a buying team where people have different roles in the decision-making process. To sell to a buying team effectively, you must know about each team member and what might influence their decision.

 **Secret Eleven — You Don't Have to Have ALL the Answers.**

One of the biggest fears that non-salespeople have is that they won't be able to answer every question a potential client might ask. They think that until they have it ALL worked out, they can't possibly go and talk to a client.

A great salesperson knows that they will never have all the answers.

Here's a simple way to confidently answer questions when you don't know the answer.

1. **Tell them you don't know.**
   **Number One Rule:** Don't try to guess or tell the person that you know. People have very good lie detectors. They will see it a mile off. Without trust, you have no sale.

   Say: *"That's a great question. I haven't heard that before."*

2. **Tell them the plan.**
   Have a plan of attack about how you answer questions like this. Be specific about what you are going to do and by when.

Say: *"Let me write that down. I am going back to the office now and will do some research for you and get back to you by _____. Is that ok?"*

3. **Clarify.**

    If numbers or details are involved in the question, ensure you get all the details written down before moving on.

    Say: *"Let me make sure I get the right answer for you – can I just clarify what you mean by _____? Can you help me with the exact numbers or details?"*

4. **Send them an email.**

    When you return to the office, send them a follow-up email thanking them for the meeting and listing the items you had to get back to them on and by when.

5. **Get them the answer.**

    As soon as you have the answer, get back to them. Make sure that you check in with them to ensure that what you've given them answers their question. This is another opportunity to uncover any more questions they might have.

    Say: *"When we met on _____, you left me with a question on _____. Here's the answer to that _____. Does that fully answer your question?"*

    Say: *"Are there any other questions that have come up that I can help you with?"*

There is a lot here to try, so take the next 11 days (or less) to choose at least one to try out for size each day. Your sales style is just that, yours.

Just like finding your style in clothing, you learn from trying things on and watching what others look and sound like. These experiences will help you amalgamate the way you want to deliver in your style. It doesn't happen overnight, but each step you take and thing you try will surely add to your understanding and the adoption of your style.

I really hope there is something in this chapter that inspires you to take action.

The next chapter will help you think about this more. Focus your actions on your clients and what they want from you.

CHAPTER 4

# What Are You Really Selling?

"A baby has brains, but it doesn't know much. Experience is the only thing that brings knowledge, and the longer you are on earth the more experience you are sure to get."

— L. FRANK BAUM, *THE WONDERFUL WIZARD OF OZ*

## Salespeople Aren't Born.

The BIGGEST problem I see when coaching business owners is this statement: "I'm not a salesperson." To that, I say, "Rubbish!" There is no such thing as "a salesperson". That is a myth devised by the crocodiles.

The truth is that everyone can and does sell. If you have ever convinced someone to see a movie you wanted to see or try that new flavour of ice cream. If you have ever achieved the major feat of getting your kids to do what you wanted – that is selling.

There are only two rules in taking on your role in **Great Selling**:

1. Be yourself.
2. Get over yourself.

## Be Yourself.

Being yourself means embracing your introversion, analytical side, storyteller, nerdiness, and passion or shyness. Be unapologetically you. There is no one way to sell that is defined by a style or personality. **Great Selling** is about authenticity and trust. When you are yourself, people will believe what they see and hear, which is how your message will get through to them. Being you builds trust in you and what you are saying.

## Get Over Yourself. Selling Isn't About You.

Getting over yourself means putting your fears and ideas about what selling is to one side and working out how **you** want to connect with your client. There is something partly frightening and partly liberating about putting your true self out in front of clients. Try it.

Sales is a practice; it is a way of getting into the client's mindset and understanding their view on what they want to see and hear. The only way to work this out for you and your client is by practising this with them.

## What is Great Selling?

**Great Selling** is a dance for two (or more). You can learn only so much from watching others or mapping it out on paper. When you dance with someone, the intersection of what you do together creates the dance. And I promise you, once you start the dance and see how it works, you will get intoxicated by the art of the dance of sales, and you will love it.

**Great Selling** is about taking your client on a journey. A journey that helps **them** make a good buying decision for **them**. When you think about it this way, making it about you is the antithesis of **Great Selling**. Whether your style is bravado, shyness, or anything and everything in between, it doesn't matter. Your job is to focus on your client and not on yourself.

> "People do not buy goods & services. They buy relations, stories & magic."
>
> SETH GODIN — THE HISTORY OF MARKETING

Your clients aren't looking for more stuff, they are looking to solve a problem and get something useful that helps them. This is becoming truer as business and personal consumers become increasingly sophisticated, educated and wary of scams and crocodiles.

There is also something liberating about making the sales journey theirs. It doesn't feel like a sham show. It automatically becomes less "pushy" and more like helping. I love seeing this mindset change in my clients – because I know the rest of the sales process flows once they start on this path.

Here's a great way to remember that it is the client's journey and their story. You are Glinda, the Good Witch of the North. It's your job to get them to start their journey on the Yellow Brick Road and not to walk it for them. To do this, you need to build a relationship, tell them relevant stories and show them the magic of what working with you can do for them.

## Connecting With Your Passion

Throughout this book, you will see me talk about stories. For your client, the person listening to your stories, there is something inspiring and attractive about seeing the light shining in someone's eyes when they talk about their business and what they do.

Stories can portray a similar problem and solution to theirs. This is an absolute comfort to them as they listen and talk to someone who lets them know that they are okay and that there is a solution and a pathway to what they want.

For you, telling your story and what inspires you is easy and fun. (Well, at least once you get used to it). Once you get your story organised (see Chapter 9 for more on this) and start telling it and seeing the response you get, there is something quite magical about it. It becomes easy to tell, and the more you tell it, the easier it gets.

Have you ever heard someone talk about their business and think, "Wow, she is talking directly to me!" When you deeply understand your client, their pain, what they really want, their fears, and hopes, you turn this knowledge into words and phrases that they would use about themselves. You will attract them, and they will connect with you. I call this your Lean-In Factor (also in Chapter 9).

## Your Client Is Scared!

Suppose you think about Dorothy when she first landed in Oz. She was terrified. She was the first woman to have a lead role in a movie; she was paid fractionally more than Toto, and it was the first time they had gone from black and white to Technicolour. As I have mentioned earlier, Dorothy was in a place she had never been; she had killed someone, and weird little voices were twittering around her. When I put myself in that scene and think about it, it amazes me that Dorothy even ventured off her front porch.

As you assume your role as Glinda, that's your first job – getting your client off their front porch. You don't have to tell them about flying monkeys, that the Wizard is a fraud, or that a Wicked Witch wants her dead. You know these things, but you don't tell her that.

You share with her that she is safe and should put on those pretty ruby slippers and come and meet the friendly, twittering voices.

When leading the sales dance, we first start with the basic steps. We want to get the client moving or even just walking onto the dance floor. We don't start with the most complicated steps and movements because that will frighten them off. Not because those movements aren't necessary or part of the dance, but because your job is getting your client to know **they** can do the steps.

It's not about you and what you can do. It's about your clients and how you can guide them through their aspirations and fears along the Yellow Brick Road to find their truth and solution.

## Connecting With Your Client.

Some things are important to your client. Sometimes they are logical and understandable, and sometimes they aren't. One of your first jobs connecting with your client is mapping these out. Who is your client? What are they interested in? Are they extroverted or introverted? What motivates them more – pains or gains and which particular pains and gains are their motivators?

One of the games I play when I first meet a new client, is to find out something personal about them. It might be as simple as when they usually wake up, start work, or something more involved. Here's my favourite example: I once met a CEO exploring a technology I was selling. By the end of the first meeting, I knew that he was one of three brothers, that his parents were missionaries and that he spent many of his pre-teen years aboard a boat sailing around the South Pacific with his family. His parents visited the islands, and the boys went along with them. You can imagine some of the things they might have encountered. How fascinating!

I get these stories from my clients because I love people and stories. Everyone has a story. This helps me get to know them, how they tick and what's important to them. I do this so that when I start talking to them about my business, product, or service, I can relate my story more closely to them and who they are.

As I mentioned, you will learn more about stories in Chapter 9.

## Going Deeper to Understand Your Business.

Before you can tell stories, you have to figure out what people think and trust about you and what you do. Building trust in your business goes far deeper and wider than understanding what people want and having some stories and social proof. Trust is built over time through consistent, clearly targeted, positive interactions that meet your client's logical and emotional needs.

We have all heard people say that we buy from people we **Know, Like and Trust**.

When I work with clients on understanding and building trust for their business, I like to pair this saying with Simon Sinek's "The Why of Business". In his TED TALK *"How great leaders inspire action"*, he uses three concentric circles (he calls The Golden Circle) that talk about business in this way:

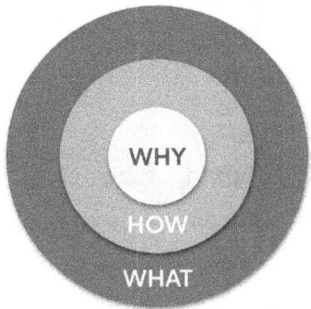

- The outer circle is **WHAT** you do.
- The next circle is **HOW** you do it.
- Centrally, and most importantly, is **WHY** you do it.

This is how I use the quote and the formula from Simon Sinek together.

- People **KNOW WHAT** you do
- They **LIKE HOW** you do it
- But they **TRUST** your **WHY**.

## People Buy From People They Know, Like and Trust.

This is one of those sayings that everyone knows and says, and we all agree it is true, but do you know how to apply it in your business? Just saying it isn't enough. Trust is deliberately built.

I have been thinking a lot about this lately and have developed some great ways of helping you rethink and apply *Knowing*, *Liking* and *Trusting* in your business. Let's get into action!

## People Buy From People.

The act of trading or selling and buying is very human and has been around forever. The first thing to focus on is that people buy from people, not from computer screens, emails or websites.

There are two parts to this. Someone has a product, asset or skill that is valuable and needed by someone else. The other person has a need, requirement or problem they want fixed.

The first person not only has this skill or product but must be aware of its value and be open and willing to share or trade it. They need to have the mindset that they have enough to share and then take the actions that make this trade possible.

The second person is searching for a solution to their problem, and they might not know exactly what that solution looks like or how to find it. But they are keen to do something about this problem. It has to be important to them.

These two people then meet to share ideas on what they have and need and work together to decide whether a trade can happen.

> **ACTION:** How do you describe what you do so that it is easy for other people to understand?
>
> **ACTION:** Where do you go to meet the type of people who have the problem you can solve?
>
> **ACTION:** How do you interpret what people want and show them you want to help them and how you can help them?

## People Buy From People They KNOW.

Knowing begins typically from the outside – people know what you do. They may know this from your title, your website or the qualifications you hold. Do people know and understand what you do?

There is a trend to make the description of what we do elegant or interesting. Let me give you an example. An accountant might describe themselves as a wealth manager. In the first instance, a person wants to know what you do and understand if you can help them. The known component is about **WHAT** you do. Think about this. If I asked you, "Do you know an Accountant? Then, a few people may pop into your head.

This is just like the door to a shop; allowing others to know and open the door is the simplest part of this equation. The thing to concentrate on with this element is to keep it **SIMPLE**. You want to make it super simple for those walking by to know what you do.

> **ACTION:** Think about how easy you make it for people to **KNOW** what you do.
>
> **ACTION:** How can you simplify it?

## People Buy From People They LIKE.

Have you ever entered a shop where the assistant doesn't acknowledge you or say hello? How does that make you feel? It makes me feel like walking straight out again – and often, that's precisely what I do. The opposite is true; you want to feel welcomed and seen but not set upon.

People like us because of **HOW** we do the things we do. How you treat them, make them feel, and help them. It follows then that to ask someone to like you and your business; you have to be open about the **HOW** of your business.

Not everyone is going to like you, and that's okay. The important thing is to know who your tribe is and how they like to interact and then build your business and your processes around them. You can't be everything to everyone, so knowing who you are serving and building the HOW you serve around them and how they want to buy is critical to your success.

> **ACTION:** How do you get people to engage with and get to know you?
>
> **ACTION:** Get to deeply understand who your target client is and isn't.
>
> **ACTION:** Get to know **HOW** your target client wants to buy from you and focus your business practices on that.

## People Buy From People They TRUST.

This element is the hardest, the deepest and the most powerful. What makes you trust someone and invest in their business over someone else's? It starts with the **WHAT** and the **HOW** you operate in business, but there is something deeper, something more important.

There is a magnetic force that draws people to you – it's trust! People will trust you and be drawn to you when they get **WHY** you do what you do.

When you allow people to understand the motives and inspiration behind you and your business, you allow them to build trust in you and your business. It is your **WHY** that draws people to you and allows you to inspire them to work with and buy from you.

In the end, transactions happen because your clients feel they can understand and trust **WHY** you are doing this, **HOW** you do it and finally, **WHAT** you do.

> **ACTION:** Think about what gets you out of bed in the morning. What is it that drives and interests you about what you do?
>
> **ACTION:** Practice describing this simply to people. You will know you have it right when you see the light in the other person's eye.

## People Buy From People They KNOW, LIKE and TRUST.

If you want to put this into action in your business, it starts by connecting with people. The secret is to allow people to easily know **WHAT** you do, **HOW** you do it, and most powerfully, **WHY**. When your **WHY** is persuasive, your **HOW** suits them, and you have **WHAT** they need, people will buy from you.

Trust is such an essential ingredient in how you build your business. In the next chapter, we will explore this in more detail.

Let me end this chapter with a story. I worked with a client whose background was as a CFO (Chief Financial Officer) for some big companies. He had just started a new chapter in his career as a Virtual CFO, advising mid-sized businesses. He went from being in charge of a team of finance people and discussing matters with the board to being in front of clients who ran their own businesses. Very different.

Finance is about numbers, yes. But — business owners start their business for a reason. Each one has their own set of ambitions, motivations and fears. There is no point in talking about the numbers without finding the relevance to the person you are working with.

Business is about people. The numbers (in this case, finance) help the people understand more about their business. But to do that, we need to capture their attention, and we do that by first listening and then relating the numbers to them.

## Go and Listen!

If you accept it, your mission is this: Go and find out what you are **really** selling. Not what **you** think, but walk a mile in your client's shoes and discover their emotional, logical and tactical journey in buying from and working with you.

In your mission, take, make and build trust. Keep trust as your North Star.

The next chapter is all about **Trust**.

CHAPTER 5

# Let Trust Guide Your Sales

"There is no place like home."

— L. FRANK BAUM, *THE WONDERFUL WIZARD OF OZ*

Experience in our lives and businesses is an essential guide to how we should continue. Remember that whilst you know a lot, this client and this experience are unique. It deserves your respect and attention – this is how to build trust.

Trust is such an interesting thing and has always been a focal point of my work in the sales arena. Trust is mercurial and brilliant. Mercurial because it is so easily broken or marked by what we do and say. Brilliant because when you see the "light" of trust in your client's eyes, you know this will deepen your relationship and bring new ideas, thoughts and fears to the forefront of your conversations.

Dorothy trusted Glinda. She also helped others trust in following the Yellow Brick Road through her journey. In the end, she and her co-journeyers found that they could, ultimately, trust themselves and their Strength, Heart, Brains, and Courage.

The last chapter examined the well-known saying: "*People buy from people they know, like, and trust.*"

In this chapter, I want us to dig into trust and how this must be the focal point of your **Great Selling** activities.

Building trust should be your priority and something to always keep at the forefront of your mind when dealing with clients. They won't buy from you if they don't trust you, your product, and your business.

The good news is that trust has an equation so you can better understand how to build it into your business. Here is my view of using the trust equation in the sales arena to build trust.

$$\text{Trust Equation}^2 = \frac{\text{Credibility} + \text{Reliability} + \text{Intimacy}}{\text{Self-Orientation}}$$

I have found from working with business owners around trust that each element (Credibility, Reliability, Intimacy) is increasingly harder to achieve – and – when used effectively, they can create deeper and greater degrees of trust.

Increasing trust opens up new and better conversations that will help you better understand and serve your clients.

Credibility and the first elements of reliability are table stakes. You must weave reliability and intimacy into your business practices to develop trust.

This chapter helps you think about each of the elements of trust and how you can implement these in your business.

## Credibility.

Most people start businesses because they are technical experts or have specific knowledge, which gives them credibility. We are generally good at showing this by having letters after our name or information on our qualifications in our marketing materials. Our associations with organisations, clients, or authorities can also show credibility. These are all examples of rational credibility; it shows people they can trust you to deliver.

There are two components to credibility: rational and emotional. The rational component is relatively easy to deliver and maintain. As mentioned above, it starts with your qualifications and builds as you answer questions about what you do and how you do it. Emotional credibility is much harder to deliver and for clients to judge. Emotional credibility is based on their perception that you are telling the truth. This element is squarely in the eye of the client. And it will be complicated by their past dealings with others. It is important to ask questions about their past experiences so you can uncover and deal with unspoken or unconscious fears and biases.

Here is a way to think about and address these fears (when they come up):

1. Clearly explain people's most common fears in dealing with your industry and how you are different or have overcome these.
2. Ask your prospective client about what has gone right and wrong in their past business dealings. Address these in your interactions.
3. Think about fears you have helped clients overcome and how you have addressed these.

Sales stories are a great tool that can help your client make up their mind. Talking about the problems and fears other clients have had and how you have helped them helps normalise the fear for the client and shows how you have helped people in their positions. The added advantage of doing this is that once you have successfully addressed one fear or concern, your client is more likely to feel comfortable sharing other concerns.

### Six Tips for Building Credibility:

1. Tell the truth.

2. Be yourself.

3. Be prepared. Show your client that you have done your research into who they are

4. If you don't know the answer, say so. Let them know how you will get the answer to their question and when you will get back to them.

5. Have a picture of your ideal client. If they don't fit, be honest and say so. This allows you to help them find someone who does or review their fit with your ideal client model.

6. Think about the informational and emotional needs of your client. Look at ways to meet these in your meetings.

## Reliability.

The second element in building trust is reliability.

Understanding reliability is simple. **Do what you say ... and say what you do!**

Most people are good at doing what they say, especially if you make notes and remember to read them afterwards.

People get unstuck by not saying what they do. We are often such experts in our field, so unconsciously competent in what we do, we simply miss the steps. We forget all the steps taken and then assume that our clients know the steps it takes. Doesn't everyone?

Think about driving a car. When you first learnt to drive, you were conscious of each step – mirrors, seatbelt, clutch, accelerator, etc. As you went on, you became less mindful of each step, even though you still do them. It is the same in your business. You are so familiar with all the steps you do every day that they become seamless to you. But for someone new, like a new client, this is foreign territory.

This is why I encourage you to stop and take a client's walk through your business. Remember you are Glinda, and it's your job to help them walk that Yellow Brick Road —more on this in Chapter 7.

Reliability is about people's perceptions of you. This starts with client referrals, testimonials, and, of course, your first interactions. After that, with each new client, it is built over time through your words and actions. With each positive interaction they have with you, the more reliable they will judge you to be.

There are obvious elements to reliability, such as getting back to people when you say you will and honouring your offers. The less obvious are the subconscious influences and how people **feel** about your reliability. For example, can you anticipate the client's needs and routines? If done well, this is a very powerful way to build reliability. Observe what they do, ask about your client's preferences, and then deliver based on those.

Here are some questions to help you with this:

- Do you prefer being called in the morning or afternoon?
- Would you prefer I send the proposal before I come and visit you to discuss it?
- Is there anyone else in the organisation that I should speak with so that I can better understand how to address this problem?

Here's something interesting about reliability. Let's say you meet with a client and tell them you will get them a proposal. In their mind, they will set a due date for that. It might be tomorrow, next week or next month. If you fail to deliver to their timetable, even though you are unaware of what it is, they will think you are unreliable.

The easiest way around this is to always end a conversation or meeting with clear next steps and, most importantly, when these will be done. They will think you are more reliable by setting an explicit delivery date and then delivering on that.

**Tips for Building Reliability:**

1. Be clear about what you intend to do and when, and deliver on these commitments.

2. Send follow-up emails of what you have discussed and your commitments.

3. Be organised. Send requests for future meetings and confirm the day or week before the meeting.

4. Ensure you know the goals of your client.

5. Ensure your client is clear on your goals.

6. Look for and respond to your client's unspoken logical and emotional needs.

## Intimacy.

Intimacy is the most important element in the numerator of the Trust Equation. Intimacy is when your client is happy to talk to you about sensitive issues or personal ideas. They can deeply want this, or it might be about an emotional connection with the problem or solution.

Building intimacy increases what you know about the person, which is a risk for them and you. Be careful when approaching people with intimate questions. They will give you answers when they are ready to trust you. You need to test the water to know if you are there yet. Intimacy is a dance conducted by asking probing questions that give the other person the space to answer or avoid.

Here are some examples of phrasings that might be used to build intimacy:

> *"Bob, it looks like you aren't happy with your existing provider. I want to be able to show you that we are different. Would you mind sharing with me why you are leaving your existing provider?"*

> *"Some clients that we work with have a similar problem to you. They tell me it frustrates them that they can't control that part of their business. Do you feel the same way?"*

Intimacy is mutual and developed by taking risks and showing your rational and emotional hand first. The adage "you have to give to get" applies here. How this applies to trust is that you are asking them to give you information, so you have to start by first giving information. When you make this information of a personal or aspirational nature, it increases the likelihood that they will respond in kind. If you risk divulging something intimate, the other person will generally feel more comfortable reciprocating.

This is true for non-trust areas. If you start a conversation about football, then the standard etiquette in conversation is to respond about football or another sport. Humans are wired this way. Talking about your personal experiences and those with other clients helps show that you like to build intimacy with your clients and then encourages them to do the same.

Not everyone will be comfortable with answering intimate questions. Be sure to look for signs of this in their body language and use your words to allow them to comfortably **not** divulge information.

When I think about this part of the sales dance, I like to think about it as if I were doing a painting with the client. You start by putting some ideas and questions out there and then pass the paintbrush onto them to see what they are happy to add to the painting. The result is a composite picture of their needs and aspirations and your ability to help them.

> **Tips for Building Intimacy:**
>
> 1. Be first to give, then wait for your client to respond.
>
> 2. Ask questions that aren't "normal" for your industry.
>
> 3. Ask questions that use "feeling" words.
>
> 4. Be sure to give them an out!

## Conflict of Interest.

Conflict of interest is also known as Self-Orientation. I use the broader term because, in my mind, there are business-based and personal conflicts. Conflict may be visible and invisible, real and perceived.

In building a trusted relationship, your focus should be and be seen to be focused on the best interests of the client and then on your business needs. Your needs should be secondary. In a healthy relationship, there is give and take based on the transparent sharing of the goals each person wants to achieve and where both parties help the other. Transparency leaves less room for the client to second guess you and your motives.

Some people think selling is about the "Customer is Always Right". Well, yes and no. Yes, you should listen and respect your customer. But – and it's a big but, this does not give them license to be, do, and say anything they want. A healthy business relationship has give and take and is built where all parties benefit and gain value from the interaction.

Showing customers the client orientation of your business is essential. They want to know that you listen, learn, and change with these interactions. It doesn't have to be all glossy, either. Some of the best sales stories for building trust come from the question, "*What happens when things go wrong?*"

Sharing your experiences and learning helps people see that you reflect and learn and have good reasons for suggesting that things get done in a certain way.

### Tips for Building Your Client Orientation:

- Tell sales stories about clients and other people — not yourself.

- Learn to **listen** well. Watch for non-verbal cues about how your clients are feeling and whether they are following you or you are losing them.

- Focus first on the problem. Once you think you know what it is, STOP. Check your understanding, and only then look to the solution.

- If you don't know, **say you don't know**. Explain **how** you are going to get the answer and **by when**.

- **Be transparent** about what you want to achieve.

- Be able to talk about times in your business when things went wrong, how you fixed the business problem, what you have learned from this, and how it has changed your business.

## Business-Based Conflict of Interest:

If you have a clear picture of your ideal client, then the area in which your prospective client is a mismatch to your ideal is where you or they may perceive conflict.

Conflict exists in a competitive arena when you are markedly different from the other companies they assess. For example, if you are smaller than your competitors, this can be seen as a source of potential conflict.

If you are a large multinational company needing legal advice, you will go to big city-based firms for this. There may well be a legal expert living in a country town that would be able to do this. However, large multinational companies will not buy from them.

If this is part of your sales arena, I implore you to get on the front foot. Talk about your differences and add your spin. Smaller companies can be more agile and responsive, which may get you over the line in your negotiations.

### Tips for Avoiding Conflict of Interest:

- Build a clear understanding of your ideal client and be able to describe them to others.
- If you see a potential conflict of interest, be the first to bring it up.
- Be honest. If a conflict will affect your ability to deliver, say so.

The bottom line is that being trustworthy builds trust. Dorothy was trusting and trusted. She was clear about what she knew and what her companions may find. But she didn't give them false hope. She told them that the Wizard might not be able to help them.

I encourage you to look for and build out your version of the trust equation to know what works for you and your clients. Creating trust can increase both the likelihood and the speed of the sale. So, it is worth investing in.

## Sales Techniques That Help to Build Trust.

The dance of sales and trust is built on techniques to help you work with your clients to understand them better and address their needs.

### Don't Assume!

If you think there could be or sense that there is a conflict, ask. Be upfront about your feelings and ask your potential client to do the same.

I remember I was working with a personal stylist. The first step she asked for was to come to my house and see my wardrobe. I remember, deep down, the fear I felt. I explained to her that my wardrobe is very personal. I am ashamed of some of the things in there that don't fit, have never worn, or both. Asking to see this first is the same to me as asking me to walk naked down the street. (Perhaps not quite that, but you understand where I am going here.)

She explained that looking at someone's wardrobe shows her the best way to help. I get that! But – the client journey is the client's, not yours. You have to earn the right to be taken into a private place. I suggested that first, she ask for a photo of your most or least favourite outfit, and then you both review it over coffee.

Then, by all means, bring up the wardrobe inspection. But be aware that people (like me) may still not be ready. When I encounter this, I try to use what I call two-year-old logic.

## Two-Year-Old Logic.

If you are a parent – you will know (from painful experience) not to ask a two-year-old what they want to wear today. Three hours later – you are still there.

Instead, you offer them two solutions. They feel they have a choice; you know you have given them two suitable options.

Big people are really just like children, but they have learned, most of the time, to mask their reactions. Big people want options, too. Use this when you are selling and guiding them on their journey.

Going back to the stylist – this might sound like:

> *"Thank you so much for sharing your outfits with me today. Normally, from here, the clients I work with either start with a wardrobe review or a scrapbook of their favourite styles and colours. Which appeals most to you?"*

## Feel Felt Found.

One of the best sales skills I know is acknowledging and working with people's feelings. It is important to both recognise and understand the feelings of this client. Here's a great sales technique to do just that. It's called Feel Felt Found. This is used to both engage with and understand your client's feelings. It can be used to answer objections positively or when you can sense some resistance or unspoken questions.

First, you must invite the person to let you know how they feel.

> *"I can sense some resistance. Can you share with me what you are feeling?"*

Here's how it works:

**1. "I understand how you FEEL"**

Firstly, you need to address the feeling that the client has shared with you. Validating their feelings helps them know that you understand what they are saying and perhaps some of the underlying reasons they might be bringing up this question.

Evaluating risks is a normal and vital part of their buying journey, and you want to show them that it is okay for them to feel this way AND that you are the right person to discuss this with.

## 2. "Others FELT the same way …"

You want them to know that others have felt that same way. Others you have worked with and bought from you.

Again, you validate their feelings and let them know they are not alone. You are normalising this for this stage of buying. Everybody likes to feel 'normal' and part of a normal buying process.

This leads us to the next step, explaining what the others found AFTER they bought and used your produce or service.

## 3. "What they FOUND was …"

This last step helps your client look to the future by acknowledging their fear, normalising it and then showing that others have overcome and enjoyed the benefits of your product or service. This is about telling your potential client how (in as exact terms as possible) the other clients overcame and addressed this fear through using your product or service.

Your potential client now has their fears allayed, but more importantly, you have allowed them to be open about their fears, and they understand your process to ensure issues are addressed and a positive outcome is reached.

## Using Feel, Felt, Found – Some Examples.

*I can understand why you might FEEL when you first look at this: the price is too high. Other customers have FELT the same way. But, when they started using the product and saw the savings they could achieve, they FOUND that using the _____ was the right choice for them.*

*I know you might FEEL that this _____ might be difficult to implement in your workplace. Others have FELT exactly the same way. They FOUND that by using our complete implementation guide, they achieved this successfully and enjoyed the full benefits of the product/service.*

## Where to Start?

Build some examples of what fears your clients have overcome. The best way to do this is to talk to existing clients.

Start using the stories you learn about with new prospective clients and see their reactions.

I suppose I can summarise by saying that trust is everything when selling. A trusted relationship makes things easier, faster and more advantageous to all parties. When you lose trust – then your client won't buy from you.

That's why I have dedicated the next section of this book to improving your client orientation.

# Section Two

# Taking a Client View of Your Business

You've made it through Section One – go you!

Hopefully you now know more about what **Great Selling** is and why you need to read on. We have just scratched the surface.

This next section of the book is to help you better see and know your client. Some great tools will give you invaluable insights into you, your business, and, most importantly, what your client actually buys from you. More than that, this section will help you understand their motivators and buying process.

Here's what I know about working with businesses on this. You know your business, but you don't really deeply know why people buy from you. Some will be obvious, and you will know. Some of the reasons, emotions and feelings will surprise you. Both are valuable and unique to your business and how you do what you do.

Knowing what and how your clients buy and what motivates them will help you sell more, and more importantly, it will help you build a better business.

CHAPTER 6

# Shut the Back Door!

> "Everything you were looking for was right there with you all along."
>
> — THE WIZARD OF OZ

Warning! You already know I LOVE selling. Selling doesn't stop once you have a new client. I increasingly see the bias for new stripping value from businesses. In the obsession to find "new clients" that is a hallmark of modern business, they forget. They forget all their work to get the precious clients they already have and care for them, so they don't leave.

I had a conversation with a bank the other day. They couldn't give me a competitive interest rate after being a client for over 25 years. Why? Not because I had been a long-term client but because my loan balance wasn't enough for them to warrant this.

It's all about them! How infuriating!

Do they think I will forget when I next need a loan? Do they think I won't talk or write about it?

Banks (and other big businesses) spend millions asking about customer experience using the Net Promoter Score and countless other tools but don't show care for their customers. It is lipstick on a pig. There is no point in measuring what isn't there. It's an illusion of care.

OK, rant over.

I am trying to make the point that when we are obsessed with ourselves and what we want, we miss the obvious. We do things that don't make sense. Great businesses are built around their clients. Not only new clients but also those gorgeous souls you have already sweated blood, sweat and tears to bring onboard, work with and care for.

## Shut the Back Door.

I implore you! Before chasing the shiny, new client, please look after the ones you already have.

There are three great reasons (any many more besides these) for this:

1. Keeping your existing clients onboard costs much less than chasing new ones.
2. There are latent needs in your existing client that you might be able to serve.

3. Referrals from existing clients are the easiest and best way to access new potential clients.

And – it is simply the right thing to do. It feels better because it is better.

Returning to my phone conversation with "The Bank", the person I was talking to felt awful. They knew it was wrong, but they had no power to change the story for me.

Before I take you on the journey of seeing your clients, we will start here. Where your clients are now, and where you are now. But before I do that, I want to share my experiences and explain why this is so important.

## Leaving Money on the Table.

I have more than 27 years of experience working in sales. Working in a sales team, building teams, in companies I own, and for others. In all of these, I started by talking to the people inside the business, and then I spoke to clients and listened to their concerns, questions, and needs. Very often, if not every time, I found that there were legitimate reasons why the clients weren't buying. There were clear, unfulfilled needs, and the client would happily pay to have them addressed.

When a client is dissatisfied, you must start in a different place. You can't just push a proposal under their noses, hoping they will sign. They won't. They don't trust that you will deliver and fear they are just getting into more issues and problems. You start differently. First, earn the right, regain their trust and deliver on what you promised.

These aren't just words but a document with clear actions and timelines. Also in this document is a request. That request is that once you have succeeded in delivering it, the client agrees to sit down with you and discuss an extension of your business together.

As I often explain to my clients, adults are just like children. Except they have learned to cover up the tantrums most of the time. Just like children, they need to have the rules of the game explained to them, and then they need to play the game fairly. And, just like children, if they are unruly, it is often just as much the parent's behaviour that needs to change as the child's. Having clear actions and holding all parties accountable for those actions are the only ways to have a peaceful household and business.

Here are the steps again on how I started and succeeded in each business.

1. Listen to the people inside the business. They will tell you the internal version of why the clients aren't buying. Often, they will tell you that client XYZ is a lost cause.
2. Listen to the clients. Go and find out for yourself. Talk to clients about their problems, what they want to buy, and what's stopping them from doing that.
3. Take this information back to the business with a proposal of what needs to be done and the returns for doing this. Get buy-in from the team and create an action plan.

4. Take this action to the client and seek their approval for the plan. Get the client to agree that once the action plan is successfully executed, they will, in good faith, enter into discussions to create and sign off on a new proposal with your business.

## Do You Have a Problem?

I am a lover of metrics. As the very wonderful Peter Drucker says, "You can't manage what you don't measure." Before you run out and talk to clients, understand where you are. Here are some good measures to understand.

**Churn rate:** What is the rate at which clients leave you? These rates alone are probably not that helpful, so a quick search will give you information on what these should look like for your type and size of business. The real point is not to get hung up on these numbers (for now). But use these as a starting point and see what you can learn from your clients about improving these rates.

Lastly, sit and review your existing clients and determine who you love to work with. Which clients are profitable, both behaviourally, emotionally and financially? Clients who pay well but give you hell are just not good business.

**Best clients:** What does your best client look and feel like, and what are their buying habits?

I implore you not to do this to justify why you shouldn't talk to clients. And don't take weeks or even days to do this. Spend 1–2 hours getting an internal starting point. There is always more money and great insights from talking to your clients. The only people who can tell you what your clients are thinking – are your clients, so get out there and talk to them.

## Warning! Don't Blame the Buyer.

Your job is to help people buy, so blaming the buyer for not buying from you isn't addressing your problem. It's part of the problem. Here's why and what to do to fix it.

People buy from you when they **trust** that you, your product or service and your business can help them fix their problem or fulfil their need. You haven't fulfilled one of these criteria if they're not buying.

Sometimes, they have logical reasons, but it is often simply a gut feeling that stops them from buying. Here are three tips on how to help your buyer buy from you.

### Seek First to Understand

Your first job is to understand your buyer. There are obvious things like finding out their problem, what they are prepared to buy and how you can help. These questions can be answered by asking and listening. Simple!

Don't stop there. You also need to understand what makes your buyer tick. Their body language, for example, will tell you about the type of person you are dealing with. This gives you clues on **how** you should go about helping them. Don't forget their feelings – get to know how they feel about your solution because everyone buys emotionally first.

## Take the Lead

Help them achieve their goals. Help them think about new ways to get there. Let them see that you can assist them. I promise they won't see you as pushy – they will love it!

Lead the client with questions and keep digging. Once you think you have a solution, lead them in exploring it and check that it will work for them and what and how they want to buy.

Lead them by being yourself and having a positive attitude to sales and your business.

## Get Intimate!

If you are going to gain someone's trust, then you have to share things about yourself and your business. Think of relevant sales stories about other clients you have helped and problems you have solved. Share these with your clients, and in the process, you will encourage them to share more information about themselves.

### Say No!

If you can't help them or they don't fit your ideal client and would better suit another provider – **say so**. Stay true to your gut feelings about which clients will work best with you, your products and your team. Sales referrals from happy clients are the ultimate sales tool; a mismatched and disgruntled client will affect your delivery ability.

Stop blaming the buyer and look at the things you can change. As Gandhi said, be the change you want to see in the world.

## Keeping Clients is Cheaper.

There are some great reasons to both retain and grow your existing clients. An old rule of thumb is that keeping an existing client is five times cheaper than attracting and converting a new one. This rule was espoused when Crocodile Selling was still in its heyday when our access to buying behaviour and other data was in its infancy.

I was reading a great article by Blake Morgan[3] in *Forbes Magazine*. Her article was based on a discussion with Wharton Marketing Professor Peter Fader, who said: "Here's my take on that old belief: who cares? Decisions about client acquisition, retention and development shouldn't be driven by cost considerations—they should be based on future value."

Yes, yes and yes.

Hmmm, I am wondering if I should send this article to "The Bank"?

There is more, though. This is just the sales and marketing spend. The root of the problem that this metric is showing is that you have a fit problem. This means a problem that their perception of what you are offering and what they want doesn't fit as well as it should.

The future value from your client is not (only) about money. It is about:

1. What they know about you and can share
2. What they might spend with you
3. What other problems/needs that you might be able to serve
4. What they have in their future
5. Who they talk to and know
6. Insights into ways you could work smarter and better to serve them.

And here is the BIG PUNCH: Intimately knowing and understanding your client will not only retain them. It will give you the "secret sauce" to attract new clients more efficiently. New clients who "fit" you and who you love to serve.

## But Wait, There's More.

A free set of steak knives. Not really, but there is more. Getting to know your clients intimately and why they buy from you is essential, but there is another, perhaps just as important reason, to go and talk to your best clients and understand what will make and keep them buying from you.

Referrals. More on this in Chapter 8.

CHAPTER 7

# Focus on Your Client

> "Fortunately money is not known in the Land of Oz at all. We have no rich, and no poor; for what one wishes the others all try to give him, in order to make him happy, and no one in all Oz cares to have more than he can use."
>
> — L. FRANK BAUM

One of the biggest mistakes (that is super simple to make and surprisingly easy to fix) is to focus on you and what you need rather than your client. Focusing on your clients, your service to them and the results they get will help you achieve your goals.

In this chapter, I will convince you why this must be your priority and give you concrete steps to take to achieve this. But know this: client focus is a muscle. The more you do it, the stronger it will get, and your business-client relationships will become faster and easier.

We all have self-centred thoughts, and they are part of our humanity. But we also know that serving others is honourable. Think of Gandhi, Mother Teresa, and John F. Kennedy.

Take John F. Kennedy's most well-known words and change them (a little).

> "Ask not what your client can do for you. Ask what you can do for your client."

## Meet Dorothy, Your Client.

Nothing is more wonderful than when someone trusts you and agrees to walk with you through finding a solution to a problem. That's what **Great Selling** is all about – assisting your client in walking their journey.

To walk with them, we have to start from where they are. Let's explore that.

### It Starts in Black and White.

Your client has genuine and transparent fears and needs. They are black and white. They have good characters who help and support them and bad ones who show them their fears in stark reality.

Your job is to help them explain these to you. Start at the surface – what is their problem? They don't want to lose Toto. Simple and concise. Start where they are. Walk with them.

## There is a Storm.

Often, when people decide to do something about their problem, it is because they have had some storm (big or small) that has motivated them to take action about their situation. The storm has real meaning and context to them. Battling the storm has a perceived outcome that they like. Your first job is to find out what has happened to bring them to this point today, where they are talking to you.

## They Find Themselves in Technicolor!

They have just stepped out of black and white and into full colour. Be gentle, this is a shock for them. Dorothy, your client, is afraid and intrigued at the same time. If we throw in strange noises from people she can't see and then, the clincher, someone's legs are sticking out from under her house, no wonder she doesn't want to get off the porch. She's frightened.

When you find yourself in a foreign place – what do you want? Someone that you trust who says, "Welcome. Don't be afraid." This is your role to help introduce Dorothy to Oz.

## Here Are Some Questions to Ask for Your Business:

1. What do you do when you first meet someone to show they are welcome?
2. How do you show them that you know this terrain and they don't need to be afraid?
3. How do you invite them to start on their journey down their Yellow Brick Road?

## Enter Glinda, the Good Witch of the North.

Glinda is serene and beautiful, calm and wise. She shows Dorothy and the people of Oz that they don't need to be afraid. She shows them the good that has come from the storm, and they burst into song in response. Both parties see that there is nothing to be afraid of.

Glinda listens to Dorothy and what she wants to achieve. She tells her how she might go about doing that. She doesn't give her the whole story, just the first bite-size chunk. Follow the Yellow Brick Road.

She makes it seem achievable and real, something that Dorothy can do in a foreign land. Just one foot in front of the other.

You are Glinda. Don't bamboozle your Dorothy with flying monkeys, fields of opium or that the Wizard is a fraud or tell her that there is another Witch who is trying to kill her. Ask her if she wants to take that first step on your Yellow Brick Road.

## Get Your Client Goggles On.

Client goggles help you focus on your client and their needs. Remember, in Chapter 5, we talked about trust. One of the things that undermines trust is self-interest. Have you ever been in a buying situation where it was clear that the salesperson had that glint in their eye that it was all about them and what they wanted? How did this make you feel? This is self-interest at play. It destroys trust.

The thing is that even though you might not think you have that "glint", if you are under stress, feeling like you desperately need that client, then you may develop that glint without even knowing. So, the next part of this chapter is how to recognise and deal with the "glint".

## Conflict May Be Visible and Invisible, Real and Perceived.

In building a trusted relationship, your focus should always be and be seen to be focused on your client's best interests.

That doesn't mean you don't get to represent your business needs, but these are secondary. In the first part of your relationship with your client, your job is to seek to understand. Understand them, their motivations, emotions and goals. In doing this, you learn to understand them and see if this client will be a good fit for your business.

In any healthy relationship, give and take are based on the transparent sharing of each party's goals. So that both parties can help each other achieve them.

Being open about what you want and asking probing questions about what your client wants is critical. Without these first steps and without building transparency, your client will second-guess you and your motives. More importantly, it leaves you with a murky picture of who your client is, as well as their motivations and problems.

## Build Your Sales Roadmap.

The Sales Roadmap is just like the Yellow Brick Road. It is a simple and effective sales tool that helps you stay in control of the sales process with new clients. Its job is to **help your client understand** a typical engagement with your business and give you a map to follow.

## Why It Works for You.

The purpose of the Roadmap is to give you a tool to show prospective clients the best process for engaging with your business and the stages that happen before, during and after the sale.

It lets you lead the conversation and clarify what they should expect from you and what you need from them. It is a touchstone that gives you comfort and confidence.

## This Works Because:

- It gives you an agenda to follow and adds consistency to your sales process.

- It is transparent for the client.
- It sets up the best way for clients to engage with you.

## Why It Works for Your Prospective Client.

### People Buy When:

- They trust you.
- They can see that you can help them.
- They understand and are comfortable with **how** that will happen.

When you first talk to a prospective client, **they are afraid** you aren't being transparent or honest about what you do and how you do it. I am not saying they are shaking in their boots, but at the beginning of an engagement, there are always questions about whether they can trust you, your business, your product, or your service to deliver.

**When you first present the client with a clear roadmap**, it allows them to see what you do and how you engage with them. This answers many of their questions and enables the client to ask questions about the process. There is transparency in this approach that says we have nothing to hide. It is also clear what will happen before you ask them to buy.

## What to Have in Your Roadmap.

Your Roadmap should cover all the essential steps a typical client takes when engaging with your business. There are three main phases:

- Pre-engagement (the sales process through to agreement to engage)
- Delivery of product/service
- Post-delivery relationship.

As always, when creating your Roadmap – construct it through your client's eyes, then road-test it with an actual client to ensure you have it right!

## But Wait, There's More!

Your client's journey is not just logical. It is logical, tactical and emotional. Be on the lookout for these elements in each step as you walk through this journey with them. These insights are gold! They enlighten you about the real reasons people buy and are motivated to take each step in the journey.

Remember, your job is to help your client buy. So, like a good Sherpa, you must know what they need on that journey and have the tools, stories and answers ready at each stage.

This transparency and guidance will encourage people to share their problems with you. The more you can enable sharing, the more you will know how to help your client.

As Dan Pink in *To Sell Is Human: The Surprising Truth About Moving Others* writes: "In the new world of sales, being able to ask the right questions is more valuable than producing the right answers.[4]" Funnily enough, I have also found that the first person I must question is myself to ensure I take an open and curious attitude into meetings. This attitude helps create the right atmosphere and attitude to really get under the client's skin and understand their needs, wants and fears.

Here's something I know from first-hand experience. Whenever I work with someone to focus on their client and map out that journey, there are wonderful, profound and often surprising insights. These insights help you sell better and build your business and delivery around your client. This makes everything in business easier. Better still, your client, your team and the world will thank you for this.

In the sales landscape, it allows you to match your actions, stories and evidence to your client and their motivations. Your best client will engage with this material, and you will find the whole sales process easier and more gratifying. Can I say it yet? Sticking with and repeating this pattern over time will turn your fear of sales into pure love.

## CHAPTER 8

# Sales is a Numbers Game

> No thief, however skillful, can rob one of knowledge, and that is why knowledge is the best and safest treasure to acquire.
>
> — FRANK L. BAUM

Sales don't happen in a vacuum; they happen when we are talking to the right people about what they need and what we can provide to fulfil that need.

One of the things that the Crocodiles have right is that sales is a numbers game. But I ask you to use this knowledge and do the work by focusing on serving your clients.

Here are two things I know about people and sales numbers.

1. Some are overwhelmed by the number of people they need to talk to. They think about all the steps and all the things they need to do. This saps their energy and takes them away from their goal, passion, and point of connection.
2. Some are so scared to talk to one person that they spend their time "doing" marketing or cleaning the house, washing ... anything other than engaging and talking with clients.

In Chapter 4, I gave you my two rules for getting better at selling.

1. Be yourself.
2. Get over yourself.

So far, I have encouraged you to be yourself. Now, it's time you got over yourself and into activity, not just any activity. I don't want you running around in circles like a mad thing. I want to help you understand the numbers that will help you focus and free you.

## Why Numbers Matter.

I remember working with a woman who had just started in Real Estate. She was working in Brighton, Melbourne – a very expensive suburb. She was wonderfully gifted at getting people to talk to her. I particularly remember one story she shared about how she got a listing from a man who was quite a recluse, living in a massive house by the beach. She talked to him about ducks. He loved and owned ducks, and they spent time sharing duck stories. When it was time for this man to sell, he gave her the listing. This was quite a coup for a woman new to Real Estate.

She gained listings, and as I worked with her one day, she became terrified. She had a meeting later that day and didn't want to lose the business. I was curious, so I asked her:

"How many houses must you auction or sell in a month?"

*"Three,"* was her reply.

"So, how many listings do you have on your books now?"

"Three ...," she hesitated. "That's it — isn't it?"

Yes. When you need three but only have three to convert, every pause, hesitation and question from your potential client is amplified. They speak straight to your fear. You will never win when you need 100% conversion.

The pressure of this is too much and means you won't be at, or anywhere near, your best. Your fear of losing one will make focusing on your client, listening and responding nearly impossible. No matter what they say, your fear sees their words and actions as moving to no, amplifying your fear.

## The Rule of Thirds.

Here is my simple rule.

One-third will say yes
One-third will delay.
One-third will say no.

So, returning to my real estate example, if you need three listings, you have nine potentials on the go. Simple!

I have used this simple and very effective metric in services, products, and all sizes of businesses. Maybe it is right for your business, and maybe it isn't. My advice is to start with this number and see how you go.

The only way to know your business's numbers intimately is to track them.

## What Numbers Do I Need?

Let's go backwards to go forward. Start with looking at your sales for the last 12 months. The most straightforward metric is to take all the clients you have worked with over the past 12 months and divide your total sales by that number. I will use some simple numbers to make my life easier and our collective brains not too stretched.

Last 12 months: 12 clients at $100 each = $1,200.

Let's use these numbers to go forward. Let's assume you want to double your revenue in the next 12 months. So, you can either double your sales to $200 per client or double your clients. Of course, other combinations and deeper analysis can be done.

I know from working with business owners that most people don't know their numbers, their average sale, and how much a client is worth over 12 months. All of these things are great things to know.

With this knowledge, you can decide what you choose to do in the future. These are decisions that we can then break down into bite-size chunks. A bit more on that later in this chapter.

If you want to get more into the numbers, here are some questions that will help you:

1. What were the number of transactions per client and the average sale per client?
2. How many new and existing clients did you work with?
3. Was there a difference in the average sale price and/or frequency with existing and new clients?

Of course, some people go to the next level on numbers, and if that helps you – go for it! If, on the other hand, you are a bit weirded out by too many numbers, then start with what you can manage. You do you!

# Where Do Your Clients Come From?

Probably not the cabbage patch! Again, let's look backwards. Don't worry if you don't know exactly – have a guess, and work with what you do know. Now is an excellent time to start tracking these numbers so that when you reread this chapter in 12 months, you can go deeper and make more informed decisions on what to focus your precious time and efforts on.

I want you to consider where your clients have come from over the last 12 months – and where you will concentrate your efforts in the next 12 months.

How many leads (warm and cold) must come through the door to achieve your target over the next 12 months?

## Warm Leads.

A warm lead is a lead that knows about or of you and what you do. They often come from a referral or have come to you based on their research. They are called warm because they are warmer. Obvious, I know! The heat is about how likely they are to buy from you.

A warm lead is friendlier towards you and more willing to share information with you. You will see from the metrics below that a warm lead is much more likely to buy from you than a cold lead. The reason for this is all down to trust (see Chapter 5).

They are friendlier because they already trust you. This trust comes from what they discovered about you from the referrer or other sources. When you trust someone, you are likelier to be open and honest about what you seek. The warm lead will share more with you, giving you a better opportunity to answer their questions and convince them that your solution is an excellent fit for their problem.

They already have a source of proof, encouraging them to give you more.

There is a great thing in our brain that we look to validate what we think. This can either work for you or against you. When we think something, our brain tries to reinforce that with what we see and, more importantly, how it interprets it.

> "Change your thoughts and you change your world."
> — NORMAN VINCENT PEALE

So I encourage you when you have a warm lead to be bolder in your questioning and your ideas so that you can help them. This will help both of your brains find a better outcome.

## Cold Leads.

A cold lead comes to you without much introduction or information on both sides. Simply put, they trust you less, so you must work harder to build and maintain that trust. This means cold leads take longer to win, are more likely to take longer at each stage, and have more stages in their buying journey.

You might remember from Chapter 6 that this is precisely why I work my hardest in the first months in a business to develop existing clients and actively ask for referrals. Sales to existing clients and referrals are quicker and easier. So, it makes perfect sense to start there.

## How Many Leads?

The honest answer is I don't know, and it depends. Each business is different. You have different offerings, pricing, and ambitions. Reflect on your last 12 months. Where did your new clients come from? Use this as a guide for the next 12 months. It doesn't matter if the numbers aren't 100% accurate. Just use your gut. And, now, start tracking them.

Using the table below, put figures reflecting your warm and cold leads over the last 12 months. Then, with the target percentage, reflect on how you would like this to be and put an estimate in the table. This helps you know where to focus your efforts to produce your desired results.

|  | Actual % (last 12 months) | Target % (next 12 months) |
|---|---|---|
| Warm leads |  |  |
| Cold leads |  |  |

I encourage you to start tracking these numbers now so that you **know**, in more detail, what your numbers are. There is real power in numbers. This knowledge gives you evidence and information on what works and doesn't and where you need to put your efforts.

## Is That Enough?

Let's look at how many leads you need to come through your door to get new clients on your books.

| Lead Type | Through the door | Qualified | New Clients |
|---|---|---|---|
| Cold | (5:1) | (3:1) | |
| Warm | (3:1) | (2:1) | |

Remember earlier in the chapter, we talked about your success rate with cold and warm leads? Well, this is where that truth comes out. I work these figures backwards.

Say you want ten new clients, five from warm and five from cold leads. Using these rough metrics that would mean:

- 10 warm and 15 cold qualified leads.
- 30 warm and 75 cold leads through the door.

Again, I encourage you to use your memory and a piece of paper to think about these statistics for your business.

## Do They Qualify to Be Your Client?

A qualified lead means that they are qualified to be your potential client. There are two sides to qualification – yours and theirs.

The first factors to consider are do they:

1. Have a problem that you can solve.
2. Want to work with you and are engaged in the process.

Once you have these, to work through the qualification process with them, you must have the following three factors in play:

1. You are dealing with or have early access to the decision-maker.
2. They have an idea of the time frame for their purchase.
3. There is a budget for this, or they are prepared to pay.

A qualified lead shows you through their words and actions that they are engaged in the process. They show you that they are ready to start down your Yellow Brick Road and will be committed to sharing the journey with you.

The end of the road isn't a prospective client saying, "Yes". The end of a **Great Selling** process is that they make a great decision for **themselves** and their business, whether yes or no.

**Your qualification**

Remember, in Chapter 6, we talked about your Best Client. This is where you get to check in with those criteria. Does this client fit with your best client, who will work well with you and love and respect you, your people, and your process?

I know it can be easy to take on anyone and everyone when starting a business. And this is okay, as long as you know the actual cost of this. Taking anyone can and will detract from your passion and purpose.

So, as soon as you feel able, start saying "No" to clients you know aren't a good fit for you. You and your people will thank me for this advice.

## Getting New Leads.

Before you start, remember to engage with your existing clients. They will generate new business and are a great source of referrals.

Here are just some ideas on how you might generate new leads in your business:

## Warm Leads:

- Have a referral program.
- Have a **crunchy idea** of who your **Best Client** is.
- Tell your clients in meetings that you are focusing on getting new clients.
- Have information on your website about how you get business by referrals.
- Write an article about referrals and happy clients in your next newsletter.
- Ask friends, family and staff for referrals.
- When talking with suppliers, networking, etc, remind them who your Best Client is.
- Have a rewards program for referrals.

## A Note on Crunchy

This is a term that I often use when I am asking people to think about their clients. Don't answer the "Who is my Client?" question with a bland answer. Get crunchy. Be precise about who they are, how they feel, and what stage of business and/or life they are in. Why? Because if you are asking someone for "anyone", they won't be able to help you. However, asking for someone super specific makes it easier for the person listening to say, "YES! I know someone just like that". More on this later in this chapter.

A word of caution regarding rewards in referral programs: Sometimes, monetary referral programs can backfire. My rule of thumb when advising clients is this: the more intimate your relationship is with your clients, the **less** likely a monetary reward will work.

Think about it. Someone you deeply trust and have worked with intimately says they will pay you to refer business to them. How would that make you feel? People who trust you at this depth don't need money to refer you to others. They just need to be asked. The money is actually a disincentive as it feels wrong or dirty. By all means, say thank you once you get the referral. So, my advice is to use monetary rewards sparingly. Try other things first.

## Cold Leads:

Cold leads are about bringing people into your orbit. This is where marketing is key. But there is also a role for sales, especially when your required numbers are small.

- Sales focus:
    - Get on the phone and call your Best Client (more on that in Chapter 9).
    - Direct Mail your ideal client to offer them help with a critical concern.
- Free Marketing
    - Network: go where your ideal client interacts offline.
    - Go where your ideal client interacts online.
- Paid Marketing: I would do these after you have a Crystal Clear, Crunchy idea of precisely who your ideal client is and what really motivates them to begin their buying journey with you.
    - Institute a "Pay Per Click" system through Google or others to feature your offering when people search online.
    - Advertise in places that your Best Client reads.

## Referrals are Gold!

There is a book I love entitled *Three Feet from Gold* by Napoleon Hill. It is the parable of how someone went hunting, unsuccessfully, all around the world looking for gold, only to find that the gold had been literally only three feet from where they started. This is a crueller version of "the grass is always greener on the other side."

Referrals are also known as warm leads. A referral comes to your business because they know something about you, have met you or a client you've worked with, and are ready to buy. Referrals are based on a recommendation that inspires a potential client to ask you for help with a problem or need.

They are **GOLD** because you have a higher percentage of getting them to buy from you, which means you make fewer sales calls, meetings and proposals to reach your targets.

Why, I hear you ask, do referrals have a much higher conversion rate than other leads into your business? It's simple, **it's about trust**. The person trusts the referrer, so they're more likely to trust you and what you say. Because of this, it is easier to guide them through your sales process and make them a happy client, too!

The potential client already trusts in you, transferred from the referee. Trust is essential in sales, and if you are already part way along the trust pathway, it increases your chance of winning the business, AND trust increases the speed of the transaction.

It's easier for you because you already know they have a problem you can solve. This gives you more confidence in calling and dealing with them. Confidence improves your ability to sell because people are more likely to believe in you and what you are saying.

There are some simple things you can put in place right now to build more referrals into your business, and here's the trick: **Be Proactive**. It is your job to ask your clients and others for referrals. This is important because someone is more likely to refer business to you if you ask.

Many business owners I talk to say this is how they want to grow their businesses, but when I ask them how they do this, they stumble. They don't have clear ideas of who their best client is. Nor do they have a structured and systematic way to ask for and respond to referrals.

### Step One — Get Crunchy.

Your first job is to get crunchy on the target client you want in your business.

This is the first step because when you ask people for referrals, they can give you someone that matches your best client. More importantly, it lets them clearly understand who you are looking for and what value you provide them.

Think about your best client as a person. Give them a name. Describe everything you can about their age, gender, location, likes, dislikes, years in business, problems they might have, and words they may use to describe these. Let's call him "Bob".

Now you are ready to take "Bob" to the streets.

### Step Two — Shout it Out!

Now you know who "Bob" is, let **everyone** involved in your business (internal and external) know who "Bob" is and that you want to find more "Bobs".

By letting people know who your ideal client is, they are better able to spot a "Bob" and more likely to remember and refer "Bob" to you when they meet him.

Start by telling everyone in your business about "Bob". They might help you create a more detailed "Bob". Take "Bob" to meet your clients and tell them you are interested in growing. Finally, take it to the streets. Think about everywhere and everyone you can talk to about helping you find more "Bobs".

You have your "Bob". Everyone knows about it. The next step is to ensure you don't forget "Bob" as you go about your day.

## Step Three: Systemise Your Referrals.

Referrals will happen more in your business when you regularly and consistently remind people about "Bob" and ask people for referrals. If you are helping people and regularly asking them to help you with a referral, they will.

In your business, regularly ask everyone involved in your business to find a "Bob". And when they do, make sure you celebrate it and let everyone know. Some companies financially reward their employees for finding "Bobs". Have somewhere to record this for each employee and department.

Have referrals clearly marked on your new client roadmap. New clients will know that you will ask for referrals once they are happy clients. Have a system to remind people about referrals when you do your regular reviews. Let them know how to refer people to you and what you will do once they have.

**Happy clients refer.**

The easiest way to get more referrals is to have happy clients – happy clients are more likely to refer business to you. If you already have happy clients, you are 80% there. Now, make it easier for them to know you want referrals. Here's an example of a way to introduce this:

"For my business, I'm focusing on getting new clients in the next 12 months. So, I'm looking for referrals. My best client is (description). Do you know anyone like that?"

Adding this one simple thing will help your clients think about people they can refer to your business, making it much more likely that they will do it.

Once you get a referral from a client, there are a few things you need to do:

- Confirm that you can use the client's name when talking to the referral.
- Make sure that you call this person and follow up on the referral.
- Keep in touch with the client about how you're going with their referral because if you're successful with them and keep in touch, they're much more likely to refer new business to you next time.

**Last thing – remember your manners.** When you get a referral, remember to say thank you. That can simply be in words. Some people choose to give money, gifts or even a nice thank you card. Find your own style.

**Not all clients are good business.**

The last thing I want to remind you of in business is that not all clients are good business. It is ok to say no to bad clients.

And the best way to do this is to really focus on your great clients – more on that in the next chapter.

•●•

## Sales is a Numbers Game.

The numbers will only free you if you know and act on them. Having them on a piece of paper or a spreadsheet you do nothing with will not bring clients through your door.

There is a great feeling about knowing how many leads you need to bring through the door. You know what mix you are looking for, and now you have some ideas about which activities you will try to attract these people.

One of my long-term clients described the liberation of the numbers. She went from fear to being able to look the numbers squarely in the eye. It allowed her brain to feel like this was possible.

These numbers over 12 months can seem big and daunting. It is best to break them down and chunk them into daily, weekly, and monthly activities so that you can allocate time in your diary to check and keep yourself accountable each day, week, and month.

As one of my first managers said: "Don't expect what you don't inspect."

### Daily and Weekly Tasks:

- Lead generation
- Following up
- Talking to existing clients
- Writing proposals
- Following up (It's here twice for a reason!)
- Answering questions
- Asking for the business
- Following up (Third time lucky ☺ – more on this in Chapter 15)

Consider when you work at your best and put your client connection tasks here. Have a number in mind for days, weeks and months. Track it. Do it and then review it.

As I said at the beginning, I don't know what your numbers need to look like. But I know with absolute certainty that your numbers will be evident in your activity once you start tracking them. They are the quartz to your seam of gold.

## Take Your Client Down Your Yellow Brick Road.

Remember, sales is a process. The journey will look after itself if you lovingly focus on each step.

For each type of sale (current client and new client), think about the steps they need (your sales process, your Yellow Brick Road) to get them through the door as a paying client. There is more detail on this in Section Three, but for now, here's a mud map:

- Getting new contacts (networking, etc.)
- How you are going to contact them (Letters/Phone Calls/Emails)
- Follow up calls
- Meetings
- Proposals
- Asking and signing up new clients.

## It Only Works When You Do It.

Getting good at selling is part practice and part "eating your greens". I know you aren't super keen and champing at the bit right now. But the only way to get better and feel better about doing this (there is a virtuous cycle at play here) is to do it. This means doing the necessary things each day and week. By all means, set up a rewards system, if that works for you, each time you achieve your numbers!

You know yourself, so do the things that you know will keep you accountable.

## Measure – Do – Measure.

Having spent nearly 20 years in IT, I greatly love the Agile Methodology. In short, this is about doing something in a sprint for a short time, reviewing and reflecting on this activity and results and then using this information to review, renew and start a new sprint.

Track your sales activities and your results when you do them. Track both the qualitative and quantitative features of your work. First, HOW you feel about what you do is relatively more important than the numbers.

What I mean by this is that I would rather you feel great and get smaller numbers through the door than get big numbers and feel demoralised or disenchanted with yourself or the types of people you are getting in.

Once we get the feeling right, we can ramp up the numbers. Find the quartz first – then mine the seam. That's where the gold is.

Here are some questions to ask yourself:

- What is my success rate on any given day or sales stage?
- Where are these from – Warm or Cold Leads?
- How did I feel, and what do I want to lean into more?

## Information Is KING.

Your success is just that – yours! Track your information on your sales success rates. This information will help you think about:

- Your conversion ratios ~ that is, how many phone calls it takes to win an appointment, etc.
- At what stage are you losing and winning potential clients, and which sales stages and skills might you need to improve?
- Once you have this information:
    - Feed it back into where you are tracking (e.g. a spreadsheet)
    - Reassess and reset your sales activity and goals.

The other key is that once your business is big enough or you choose to get a salesperson, this information will help you select and manage them because you will know what activities work for you, your business, and your best clients.

## Are You Being Realistic?

You know yourself, but my guide is to commit yourself to numbers you think are a stretch – but not unachievable! The reason for this is deeply human. When our goals are unachievable, they work as a demotivator.

You never know if you reach for the stars; you might just touch the moon. If you are overstretching yourself, aiming too high, and thinking it is unattainable, you will become disillusioned and stop your sales activities.

I need you; you need you to keep going.

## Set a Review Date

Take some time every week and month to review your numbers. I encourage you to do this with someone you trust and who will tell you the truth so you feel accountable. You can have another set of eyes and thoughts as you review your numbers.

Use this time to review what you have learned and how you will apply what you have learned to do things differently next month.

## Just Do It!

None of this will work unless you work. You will never improve unless you get out there and give it a go. You will fail, but that doesn't make you a failure. We don't look at a toddler and say each time they fall over, "That's it! They are never going to walk."

You are learning something new; you are learning how to sales walk. Give yourself a break; be both gracious and honest with yourself. But keep going.

As an encouragement, I want to share with you Sally's story. She came to me hating sales and hating the very idea of asking. She is a helper, someone who helps deeply troubled people. She does this in love and service. So, asking and "selling" felt foreign –and wrong.

One of the first things we did together was the numbers.

The numbers liberated her, giving her something to aim for and work towards. She gained confidence as we worked through the activities we will do in Section 3 of this book. She reviewed and refined her numbers.

As she spoke to others about her business, she felt it was more of a business that justified her efforts. It gave her a vehicle to talk to her husband (an Accountant) about her numbers and results, something he liked to hear about. It combined deep humanity and service with business reality in a meaningful and doable way for both of them, so much so that years later, her husband joined her in her business.

This book's next section is about getting you onto the street taking you out of your comfort zone. But I promise you – I am your Glinda, there is a Yellow Brick Road here, and on this journey, my Dorothy, you will find friends, and more importantly, you will find that the truth and the answer were always there, right inside of you. The journey is one where you will find your Best and Worst Clients. You will find your friends and enemies. In the journey, you will find your Yellow Brick Road and be able to walk your best clients through it – because you know it – brick by brick.

So, let's dig in and get out there. Sales is one of the professions you only ever learn about when you are unprepared because you **have to** work it out in front of your Dorothy.

At the end of the next section of this book, I will pass the baton (in this case, a magic wand) to you – and will deputise you to be your very own Glinda in your own story.

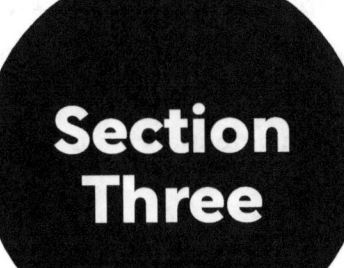

# Take It to the Streets

**Section Three**

Sections one and two of this book are just the warm-up for section three.

Selling is an art and a science. In some ways, it is very different from all other business disciplines. The only way you get better at selling is to sell. The science part can be done in the background, out of the limelight. But the art of selling must be crafted in front of a potential client.

Selling and Marketing are sisters, not twins. Marketing is something that people want to get 100% correct. They want it to be perfect as they lean into the data, art, and work. Sales is something that you have to start now with what you have. There is no waiting for a brochure, website, the right words (and the list goes on).

Selling is connecting with a person, a potential client. It is dancing with them and discovering more about them and what they hope to achieve. The dance changes depending on who you are dancing with. There are different steps needed depending on your partner. And so, this skill of being able to dance with anyone and making them look like the star of the floor – is practised. However, it has to be practised **with** potential clients.

So now is your chance.

The following chapters walk you through how to start dancing the dance of sales.

You will have successes and failures. Most importantly, you will learn from these how to dance with your clients and what skills you need to improve.

So, let's get to it! One, two – cha – cha – cha.

Like all good dance teachers, I will give you a simple process to follow.

## Listening:

**Great Selling** starts with listening. If our job is to help others make a great buying decision, we must first listen and understand who we are speaking with and their problem.

More on this in Chapter 11.

## Find the Fit

Once you have listened, only then can you see if there may be something you can help them with. This part of the sales process isn't a licence to talk endlessly about yourself. Fit is being clear about what you have heard and explaining how you can help them – using stories and ideas that **fit** their problem and business.

More on this in Chapter 13.

## Look for Objections

If you have listened to any sales training, you probably will have heard the term – handle objections. I don't like this, and I will tell you why. You handle a snake, a problem or a tricky person.

In Crocodile Selling, objections are to be squashed or batted away. And certainly not **looked for!**

Objections aren't any of these things. Objections come up in a person's mind when considering buying from you. Why would you want to get rid of these? Working through questions and ideas with your clients is essential if you are going to get a happy client.

More on this in Chapter 14.

## Always Be Creating Value

There is an old ABC in Crocodile selling. It is Always Be Closing. You should look at the first (and every opportunity after that) to close the deal and get the client signed up.

In **Great Selling**, I have changed this to Always Be Creating Value. You will know when you have hit on the gold of a Great Sales Process when there is value everywhere – for you, your clients, your team and the community.

The wonderful thing about this process is that it is cyclical. Once you have gone through it once, you get to listen some more and start the whole process again.

**CHAPTER 9**

# Clients Will Listen When You Speak to Them

> "If I ever go looking for my heart's desire again, I won't look any further than my own backyard. Because if it isn't there, I never really lost it to begin with!"
>
> — DOROTHY, *THE WIZARD OF OZ*

When I first start working with people to improve their selling, I hear things like this:

*"I don't know what to say."*
*"I am worried I will sound like a fraud – or too pushy."*

Just like Dorothy, they are looking at things all the wrong way.

Truth bomb! Here is what is going on. You may go unprepared; you go to a meeting and fail to connect with your client. You talk too much about yourself and don't listen enough. And then, you think you are no good at selling.

You are right. But – it isn't you – it's your actions. You can be part of the **Great Selling** Revolution. You just need to change what you are doing. This comes from thinking the wrong way about selling. When we think selling is icky or pushy, then we will do **anything** not to be like that. But instead of this moving you to be better at selling, it stops you.

Let me explain. When you are prepared, listen, and engage, the idea that you are no good at selling can be very simply and effectively turned around. There are three key steps in this:

1. Owning and telling your story.
2. Preparing to meet your client.
3. Be humble but not backward.

## Owning and Telling Your Story.

There is something great about owning your story in business. You are unique, interesting and passionate. Use this! Don't hide your light under a bushel. Had Glinda never shared what she knew, Dorothy might have stayed on the porch, terrified!

There is a reason why we tell our kids stories. They are easy to speak and remember for you and the listener. They speak to truths greater and deeper than us. More than that, it's fun! It shows your passion and gives you that "twinkle in your eye".

Storytelling is a great way to promote you and your business. It is an especially important sales skill for people who hate selling because stories are much easier to use. When you are telling a story, you feel more natural, and it doesn't feel like boasting in the same way that talking about yourself and your business does. It's much better than answering the question, *"What do you do?"*

Stories educate and inform. Human beings have been telling stories since time immemorial because they work. It is how we learn and understand our world and other people. Stories are memorable.

There are two key ingredients to make them memorable:

1. Content and structure.
2. How you deliver it your way.

## Content: What Is Your Story About?

Your stories should emphasise your point of difference. We covered this in Chapter 4. These are the reasons that people choose to work with you. They are essential as they give the listener insights into how you operate and work with your clients. The more you know about your prospective client and their problems, the better you can choose the story that will likely resonate with them.

When you do this well, you will have an effective sales pitch. An effective pitch isn't dramatic; it simply means that your audience and people will want to listen and know more. They want more because they have the same problem that you are describing and want to understand how you might be able to help them.

## Tell Your Audience About Your Successes.

Your successes are everywhere. You are great with your clients, especially with how you help them and the results they achieve.

- Success in starting and continuing to run your business.
- Success in helping a client overcome a problem.

When your audience has that same problem … now they are listening!

But don't stop there. Once you try these stories out, you will see the story's power and other opportunities to use them in your business. Stories can also be about:

- How clients engage with your business.
- What happens when something goes wrong?
- And many more!

## Delivery: Your Story, Your Way.

Stories are a great way to learn to sell because you can tell a story about your ideal client and how your business is geared to help them. When you deliver a story that addresses a problem your potential client is experiencing with confidence and style, they will listen. When spoken from the confidence of experience, people are more likely to trust and believe what you say.

It won't happen overnight, but it will happen! You need to take some time to create and practice your story. The best way to refine your sales pitch is to do this in front of real people. They are the ones that you want and need the reaction from.

Start in front of the mirror if that helps you, but not for too long. Your reflection, mother or partner are not who you want to buy from you. Whilst their opinion matters, it doesn't matter nearly as much as a real, live, breathing client.

Your stories are about you – but more importantly, they are about your clients and the value you have delivered them.

There is much more to stories and selling. A book that I like and recommend on this is: *Seven Stories Every Salesperson Must Tell* by Mike Adams.

# How To Build a Winning Pitch.

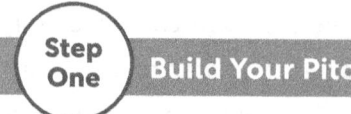 **Build Your Pitch.**

A pitch is how you tell people what you do.

The purpose of a pitch is to have people **listen to and engage with your idea**. Before you start, remember that everyone listens to WIIFM (What's In It For Me). People aren't interested in you and what you do. They are interested in how you might be able to help them solve a problem or meet a need.

- Hi, I am ... from ...
    - The problem we see is ...
    - Do you have that problem?
    - Can you explain how that affects your business?
    - Are you interested in solving it?
    - Have you tried solving it before?

Example:

> *"Having worked many years in sales and helping people sell, I find that most new business owners I speak with don't understand or are afraid of sales and selling."*
>
> *"Do you have that problem?"*

STOP AND LISTEN and explore how this affects them, their business, their teams, and their aspirations.

Not every problem is one that people are invested in solving. More than that, if it isn't in your client's top three problems, they probably don't have the headspace or financial means to solve it.

If they are interested, it's essential to understand what they have tried before and what has or has not worked. This will give you clues about a different approach to the issue or what pitfalls must be avoided.

### Step Two: Take It to the Street.

Your clients and potential clients are essential in refining your sales pitch.

The critical thing to learn is **what your clients are interested in**. As you explain to people what you do and listen to and answer their questions, you will get great insights into what problems they see, how they describe them and most importantly, what they would do about them. What you are looking for is what I call your Lean-In Factor. More on this later in this chapter.

**I cannot stress enough how important this step is.** It should be one of the first things you do with your business idea. Nothing is worse than taking something to market once you have spent time and money on it, only to discover this isn't a problem people have or want to solve.

## Step Three: Make It a Conversation.

Once you have established a connection with someone, your job is to **get them talking** so you can learn as much as possible about them, their business and what makes them tick.

Listening and asking great questions is a skill in its own right – see Chapter 11 for more on this.

## Step Four: Tell Them Your Story.

Once someone is interested in knowing more, tell them your story. Here is an example of the format I use:

1. **Experience ~ Problem**

   *"Having worked many years in sales what I find is that most new business owners don't understand or are afraid of sales and selling."*

2. **Solution**

   *"So, I decided to build Metisan to focus on sales training for people who aren't salespeople and don't necessarily understand or like sales."*

3. **What makes you different?**

   *"As I researched the market, I could see there was no sales training aimed at the great majority of people to whom sales is foreign."*

4. **What I have done about it is:**

   *"I put together a completely jargon-free sales course aimed squarely at people who know nothing about sales but need to sell. It is about debunking the myths about sales and then teaching them what **Great Selling** is about."*

5. **If you are interested in knowing more ... <asking them to buy>**

   *"The first thing I do is get to know you and your business, and I am happy to spend an hour or so to learn about you and see where I might be able to help."*

As you are talking, engaging, and listening, you need to watch which areas of the conversation people are engaging in. I call this your "Lean-In Factor". Learn from your interactions with people and use this feedback to refine your pitch. After all, your pitch is about you, but it is **for** your client.

# What's a Lean-In Factor?

I know that getting out there and talking about your business can be tough and seem icky! On the other hand, I also understand that all businesses need to find new clients. Have you ever spoken about what you do and left the audience flat? That's because you haven't found the **Lean-In Factor** for you and your business.

Your Lean-In Factor is the **secret ingredient** that will make you more comfortable talking about your business and get better results.

> The lean-in factor is that "thing" that makes people lean in (often literally) and want to know more.

## The Lean-In Factor ~ Ingredients:

**Talk about them and not you.**

Remember I mentioned WIIFM (What's In It For Me) earlier in the chapter?

When you listen to the radio and a song or information interests you, you "tune in"; once it is over, you "tune out". Your clients are precisely the same. When you say something that interests them (or is about them), they will listen or "tune in".

Consider how you can "tune" what you say to speak to their industry, business, fears and interests.

**Touch their pain point.**

You need to talk about **their pain**; what is it that is going to motivate them to do something about their problem? They are not going to buy from you simply because they like you. They will buy from you if they trust that you can deliver a meaningful solution to a problem causing them pain.

You should have noticed a **Lean-In** if you have done Steps 1 and 2 correctly. If you haven't, try again, change tack and see what your client responds to.

If you have – great, but it's not over until the fat lady sings, so keep going. You want to be able to replicate this. There is always something new to learn from your clients.

**Prove your solution.**

Your job now is to keep showing them that you know about them, their industry, their business, their pain and how to solve it. The best way to do this isn't to talk about yourself. It's to use stories about clients you have helped or things you have learned along your journey. **Stories are great because** they are:

- Easy to remember (for you and the client).
- Have a theme or moral that people will engage with.
- Show the experience of your product or service and how it works in real life.

Your stories should also show them that you are **qualified to help them.** I don't just mean you have the right technical skills. Think beyond this. Can they get along with you? Does your business style match what they need?

**Know the next step.**

The biggest mistake that non-salespeople make is to miss the next step.

At the end of the conversation, everyone should be clear about what you and they need to do next to take this discussion forward. This can be various things, depending on the size and complexity of what you are selling. Here are some examples:

- Buy from you.
- Send them some information that they need.
- Sign up for a free something.
- Have another meeting.

This step comes from Chapter 7, which discusses your Client Journey and Client Roadmap. **What's next?**

I will leave you now with the last critical ingredient.

**Practice!** You will only find your Lean-In Factor by talking to people, preferably face-to-face. Practice is essential for two reasons:

1. It will help you find your Lean-In Factor. Body language is essential in telling you how a potential client reacts to your words.
2. It allows you to refine your Lean-In Factor until you can do it confidently.

You never know; in one of these conversations, you might win a new client – and that's what it's all about!

Meetings are another opportunity to listen; being prepared helps you listen better and ask better questions.

## Preparing to Meet Your Client.

> "Luck is what happens when preparation meets opportunity."
>
> — SENECA

Knowing your clients, or at least getting to know them, is critical. Have you ever been in a business meeting where the other person has prepared? They have read about you, looked at your interests and have attempted to make this meeting add value.

You don't feel stalked or weird. You are impressed. You welcome their preparation and efforts, making you more open and kind in answering their questions. This is precisely the type of preparation that I am talking about.

**Great Selling** is about finding common ground between you and the other party. The key here is understanding what motivates your clients. Typically, this is a problem they want to solve or an ambition they wish to achieve.

Part of your research and preparation is considering who you need to target in the business. In small business, this is often the owner. In larger businesses, the decision-maker can be an employee.

Knowing this matters because who you are talking with influences what sort of information they are interested in finding out – about you, what and how you do business and how you might solve their problem.

## Why Knowing Who You Are Talking With Is Important.

When you speak with a potential client, you must give them the information they seek to influence and help them prioritise the products or services that will fit their business.

You need them to help you understand how decisions are made in their business and what's important to the decision-maker.

Typically, owners of businesses are more interested in what you can do to help them grow or overcome a growing pain they have. They are interested in efficiency, revenue, costs and risk reductions.

Employees, on the other hand, may well talk about these same things. Still, underlying this is a self-interest component about helping them save their job or promote their interests with the power brokers within the business.

Researching your clients shows that you value their time and have put effort into thinking about what they might be interested in before trying to connect. This effort is commonly respected. Even if your theories on their interest aren't quite right, they are more likely to open up and share with you because you have made an effort.

There's a great book by Sam Richter called *Take the Cold Out of Cold Calling*. He says: "Information is key to almost any sale. The more information you have on your client and their needs, the better chance you have to ensure your solutions are relevant and the better chance you have to close a deal."[5]

## Finding Out About Your Client.

The Internet is an excellent resource for finding out about your potential client by using:

- LinkedIn
- The business website
- Google.

**LinkedIn.**

LinkedIn is an excellent resource for building and using your networks. If you know someone who knows the person you want to connect with, then I encourage you to pick up the phone. Find out more about the person and some suggestions on the best way to approach them. Better yet, ask them for an introduction.

Here are some examples of questions you might ask:

- What sort of person they are?
- How do they like receiving information?
- What kind of approach will work?

I am a big fan of Jill Konrath. Here are a few of her tips on using LinkedIn to increase your sales[6]:

- Know your ideal client – Search by title and industry for the ideal contacts at your ideal customers.
- Be sure your profile is complete and contains the appropriate keywords for your business so that people looking for your solution will find you.
- Endorsements/recommendations count for a lot – get them from people who have been your clients if possible.

**Searching on LinkedIn.**

LinkedIn isn't just for looking up names that you already know. Here are some ideas on how to get the most out of LinkedIn searches:

Use Advanced Search with parameters that match your ideal client and goal:

1. Location
2. Industry

3. Function
4. Keywords
5. Browse the network of your existing clients' connections
6. Look at the groups your ideal clients are members of and review member lists
7. Search by Company or Business Name.

Once you have found a prospective client to call, use LinkedIn to find out what they are interested in:

- Look at their profile and what they say about themselves.
- What is the best way to contact them?
- What groups are they a member of?
- Most importantly, do you know someone who knows them? If you have connections in common, you can ask them to introduce you.

The more you know about this person – the better you can establish a meaningful connection.

**Company or business website.**

What you are looking for:

- People:
    - Positions and titles
    - People that you might know
    - How many people are in the business
    - What are their interests or areas of expertise
    - Photos (so you can recognise them)

- Company or Business information:
    - What do they sell?
    - What industries do they focus on?
    - What is their current news or situation?
    - Do they work with your competitor?
    - Annual reports
- Some things to do:
    - Sign up for their newsletter if they have one
    - Follow their Facebook and LinkedIn pages.

**Google.**

I use Google to find out what else the person may be interested in. Are they a member of the local football team, keen on cycling, or have other interests? Affectionately known as Google Stalking, it gives clues on the non-businessperson and their interests.

Look for:
- Articles they have written.
- Articles where they are mentioned.
- Teams or clubs they are a member of.
- Other interests that they might have.

### Google Search Tips:

Using quotation marks around the name will give you a more precise search of the whole name. Search for "Frances Pratt" instead of Frances Pratt.

Don't ignore offline research.

Look out for news in industry magazines and newspapers on your prospects or things they might be interested in. Listen for news and current affairs stories to share when you are in the car.

Talk to people. If you know someone who has worked in that industry or, better yet, with the business, talk to them to understand keywords, phrases, or approaches that might give you an edge. They will be a great source to help you better understand the culture of the business or industry.

Research helps you think about what type of person you will be meeting. What kind of approach might suit them, and which things will interest them most?

Research is also about being smart with your time and calling on people likely to need what you offer.

**It's all about fit** – fitting their need or problem with your solution. If you find a client with this, they will want to buy from you to address their need or problem.

## Be Humble But Not Backward.

There is a fine line in selling between connecting and pushing. I have seen it when someone's passion pushes a little too far. They start talking at you and about them. They forget to listen to you. But (and it's a big but) – please do not let this stop you from getting out there.

Selling is something that happens in the real world when you are speaking and connecting with people.

Here are some ideas on how to be humble and forward.

**Be clear** about what you are trying to do, the value you offer your clients and why you started your business. You had intent, a reason to start the business – and now is the time to take that through to fruition. Tell that story and engage with people to whom your value is valuable.

**Be honest** with yourself and with others about what you can do and how you can help them (or not). It is only through the exploration of ideas and sharing that you build trust with your clients. When you have this trust, and you both know that you can help, they will say yes.

**Find the win:win** in all situations. OK, you have your intention clear and your honesty hat on … so before you try to engage, make sure you have your client goggles clearly on. Review what you know about them and your hypothesis on what they want to achieve – what their scariest problem might be. It's time to show them you understand and how your wonderful talents can help them solve that!

In the next chapter, I will help you explore how to run meetings that rock your client's world (and yours)!

CHAPTER 10

# Meetings That Rock Your Client's World (And Yours)

"It's always best to start at the beginning. And all you do is follow the Yellow Brick Road."

— GLINDA, THE GOOD WITCH

Congratulations! You have organised a meeting. Now, I want to help you ensure our hard work pays off!

I know plenty of people (including myself) who get a little nervous before an important meeting with a potential client. For people who hate selling, it can be daunting.

## Sales Tips For Meeting Nerves.

I want to start this chapter with a few sales tips that I use that will help calm those nerves and start you with your best foot forward.

### Be Prepared.

Do your homework on your new client. Who are they? What are they interested in?

Know about them and what their business does. Look at their website to learn about their business and how they represent themselves. Review information on what they sell, their people, newsletters, and the words and style they use to talk about their business. These will give you insights into who they are and their personality.

Don't forget Google and LinkedIn are great tools to give you more information on their background and connections.

For those who have skipped forward to this chapter (it's ok – I do it too), look at Chapter 9 for more about preparation.

### Take Your Best Game.

What are you good at? Know how to explain what you do and how you do it engagingly. People like stories – so have your sales stories ready. We covered this in more detail in Chapter 9.

**Look good.** Take pride in how you present yourself and your business. When you look good, you feel better about yourself and automatically come across with greater confidence to the person you are meeting with.

Confidence in yourself and what you are talking about is critical because confidence assures the listener that you know who you are and what you are talking about.

## Be Early.

Don't rush in at the last minute, or heaven forbid, be late! I plan to arrive with at least 10-15 minutes to spare. That way, I can have coffee, review my preparation notes, check my emails, or just breathe.

If you are overly anxious, the other great thing to do once you are there is to close your eyes and imagine the meeting going well. Imagine yourself smiling, being introduced, and greeting people. Our imaginations are **powerful**. If you imagine what it looks, feels and smells like to have a successful meeting, then your brain wants to show you that. It will show you the information that supports your ideas and filter the data that doesn't.

## Be Yourself.

Engaging with people is all about being yourself. The best person to represent you and your business is you! As a business owner, you need to be your own sales champion!

Selling isn't only for those of us who are extroverted. It is for everyone! Be yourself. If you are quietly spoken and reserved, then be that way.

Being yourself means allowing your potential client to meet you, the real you. You come across more authentically, encouraging your client to do the same. Not only will people engage with you, but you will get more out of meetings by being yourself and being honest. The name of the game is to get to know more about their business. Being you in the meeting gives you the best chance of achieving this.

People buy from people they know, like and trust. When you are being yourself, you make both of these things more possible.

### Know Your Message.

Knowing what and why people buy from you now, in their words, is the best way to create your message. When your message is spoken in client terms in a way that your clients will readily understand, it makes it easier for them to buy from you.

If you aren't sure, then take it to the streets. Getting your current clients to help you script it is easiest. For more on this, have a look at Chapter 9.

Forget jargon, please! Nobody in the real world talks or understands jargon. Work on accurately explaining what you do and why people love working with you in "client-centric" terms.

> **Have an Easy Meeting Structure.**

You organised the meeting, so you need to be in charge. However, this doesn't give you a licence to talk endlessly about yourself. Your first meeting is about discovering more about your client. I use an excellent and easy-to-remember sales meeting structure called You, Me and the Next Step. I cover this in more detail later in this chapter.

**My promise to you:** It does get easier over time. The more you practice, the better you get. I have been selling for more than 27 years. Those butterflies give me the impetus to do my homework and perform better. You can, too!

## The Scarecrow: Your Client Doesn't Have a Brain

Before we get stuck into meeting structures, I want to take you on a journey into your client's brain.

> "Some people without brains do an awful lot of talking ... don't they?"
> — SCARECROW, *THE WONDERFUL WIZARD OF OZ*

I have sold lots of things to many different people. There is a common theme: your client doesn't understand what you sell. More than that, they are very often scared of what they don't know and are undoubtedly worried that others might know that they don't know.

It all sounds a little complicated. That's because none of it is logical. It is based on emotions — most notably, fear. Fear makes us all do irrational things; your client is no different.

If you can successfully hold your client's hand and get them to be honest about their fears, you have a fighting chance of helping them address these and buy from you. Let's unpack how this works.

## What Is Your Client Afraid Of?

**What they don't know.**

Lots of people are not only afraid of what they don't know, but they are also afraid that you will find out that they don't know. This creates a cat-and-mouse game to get to the truth.

**Here are some tips on how to address this:**

- Take an educational approach.
- Don't assume that people know what you do or anything about it.
- Let them know the outcome.

> "At the end of our meeting, you will understand _____. My job is to give you all the information you need to make an informed business decision on _____."

**The consequences of doing something.**

Because this isn't something they understand and haven't found someone they trust, they feel safer staying on their pole in the field, watching the world go by.

You must compel them to join you. You do this by waving a carrot and wielding a stick (sometimes in equal measure) to get them to understand what doing nothing means. To educate them to understand that doing nothing is worse than doing something.

**Note of caution:** Sometimes, doing nothing is a legitimate response. Be sure to give them the information so they can make the decision. No bullying (Lion) tactics allowed.

## How To Deal Positively With Fear.

The first thing to understand is that fear of what we don't know is a highly typical human experience. Whether you are selling to individuals, big companies or anything in between, fear will be there waiting to shut the door in your face.

You have to push their buttons.

It's true. If you are going to help them overcome fear, you must be upfront with them. Help them to explore their fears. Here are some tips on how to do that:

- **Name it.** Name what you see and listen carefully to the response.
- **Tell stories.** Use stories of other people's fears (that you think are relevant) about what they found and how they overcame them.

After you have pushed their fear buttons, you HAVE to apply a salve. Talk about the solution and how you can help them overcome their problem. Make it worthwhile for them to do something despite their fears.

Like the Scarecrow, our clients are smarter and more in touch than they think. Tell them what you know to inspire them into action, but be honest. Think about Dorothy. She didn't say, "Absolutely, the Wizard will be able to help you." She said that he might. They went on a journey together down the Yellow Brick Road to find out.

## What Crocodile Salespeople Do.

You can take advantage of people. When they are scared, they can make decisions that they later regret. Have you heard of buyer's remorse? You can use these tactics for evil, but I know you will use them for good. I trust you.

## Take Your Clients On a Buying Journey.

Help them experience the difference you can make for them.

> "Can't you give me brains?" asked the Scarecrow.
> "You don't need them. You are learning something every day. A baby has brains, but it doesn't know much. Experience is the only thing that brings knowledge, and the longer you are on earth the more experience you are sure to get."
>
> — L. FRANK BAUM, *THE WONDERFUL WIZARD OF OZ*

## Selling Is a Dance.

Before we talk about structures, I want to make something clear. You are in charge of the sale. You are leading the dance.

Imagine you ask someone to dance, the music is playing, you are dancing — and then suddenly you stop. The music continues, and your client, your dance partner, is just left mid-step. This confuses your clients, and they feel abandoned.

It is your job to lead the sale all the way through. Keep the music going and help them know the steps. Dance with them. Lead them. Here's how.

## Meeting Structure: You, Me and the Next Step.

This structure is one of my oldest and favourite things to share with people. It is a simple and effective sales meeting structure. I use this sales technique for meetings, phone calls, emails, and everyday life.

Before we start, we have to think about the intention of selling. **Great Selling** is about getting to know your clients, helping them understand what you offer, and assisting them in seeing the pathway that delivers value. Selling is also about influencing the other person (that doesn't mean manipulating) but positively influencing them so they will consider listening and engaging with you. **Great Selling** is helping others and finding and offering solutions where all parties win. Remember, Always Be Creating Value.

## Part One — You! (Which Is Really Them)

Remember, your client is Dorothy – on the porch. You need to start your conversation where she is to get her off the porch. If this is the first time you have met and spoken with them, this can be tricky, so preparation is vital.

Here are some ideas on where to start:

- What do you know about them?
- Who do you know that knows them?

Make educated guesses from your discovered information and what it tells you about the person you want to approach.

In your first interactions, use this information. This shows them that you have taken the time to make a serious connection by doing your homework. Show them things that you think they might be interested in.

### Warning

Be careful not to be too presumptuous. Your ideas are hypotheses. Use words like "I see from your website ...", "and so I think you might be interested in ...". Then, wait, let them tell you if you are right or wrong, and use this to explore further.

---

The purpose of **You** is to get them talking about themselves and opening up to you. This allows you to learn about them, what makes them tick and what they hope to achieve. Think about yourself as a journalist. Your job is to ask many questions and allow the conversation to go where they lead you.

Questions are their own art form; there is more on this in Chapter 11.

In any conversation with someone new – this component should take up 80% of your time or email.

## Part Two: Me (Which Is You)

Once I know more about them, and I think I can see some value in taking this further, this is where I talk about myself.

This does not give you licence to start at "when I was born" and progress through your entire life history.

Your "me" component needs to relate to what you have just learned about the person in front of you. Use what you have learned and stories and ideas that relate to what they are interested in. This is a great time to use stories and testimonials so that you aren't so much talking about yourself but what others have said about you.

Remember you are focusing here on Fit. How does your solution fit with the client's problem? This is also the time when you can say no. That there isn't a fit — if that's what you see. We are not trying to smoosh the step-sister's foot into the Glass Slipper.

Yes, this is harder to do in an email, but the same principle applies. Think about your key messages and which of these you think will resonate with this person.

This component should only be 10% of your time or email.

## Part Three: The Next Step

The next step is critical. This is often where people miss out. Missing out here makes the follow-up harder, wastes time and leaves things undone.

You now know more about the other person, and they know more about you. This is the perfect time to put out what you want to achieve from this meeting. Offer them the logical next step in your Client Journey.

One of the things that I know about sales (and in life) is that if you don't ask — they can't say yes!

When you ask, use dates and times so everyone knows what is happening and when.

Words for this:

> *"Thank you so much for today. We have covered a few great points. I can see that we might be able to help you with _____. The next step is for me to go away and prepare a proposal on this. I will be able to get that to you on Thursday. Given that I do that, when is the best time to connect with you again?"*

Get a date and time. Confirm this with them. Sometimes (particularly if they are super busy), I send them a meeting invitation for the follow-up call.

Remember – you are leading the dance. You are in charge. There are more tips on following up in Chapter 14.

---

### Warning

Be prepared for them to say no. No is okay – and it doesn't mean you have to stop. Thank them for their time, and ask them why – so you can learn for your next call or email.

---

Some words that might help are:

> "Thanks for your time. I enjoyed talking with you. Can I ask you one more question? I am approaching other people about this; would you mind telling me why this isn't of interest to you so I can learn from this for my future approaches?"

The bottom line is that you must practise and give yourself permission to get things wrong and learn from your experiences.

## A Last Word on Running Meetings.

All of these ideas are just that. The **most** important thing I want to leave you with from this chapter is to be you. Own your space and style. Here are some tips from Charlie Chaplin on just that.

> "We think too much and feel too little. More than machinery, we need humanity; more than cleverness we need kindness and gentleness."
>
> — CHARLIE CHAPLIN[7]

Is it too harsh to say that what is stifling you and your business right now is that you overthink?

The reality is that how you feel about what you are doing and what you are choosing dictates what you do and how you choose to do it, how people perceive and react and even how you interpret their responses.

Let's break down how this works (or doesn't) and then look at how to do it differently.

## Less Thinking, More Feeling.

You think you are no good at sales. This makes you feel bad about approaching people, and you then go and act on this – you feel awkward and like you are bad at selling and connecting. You choose not to be super positive about your business. You decide not to ask all the questions you know you should or to ask people to take the next step with you. The people listening to you pick up on this and then respond accordingly. You see the response (which isn't what you wanted) as confirmation that you are no good at selling. And so the cycle continues.

People connect with your heart and how you feel about what you do in your business. Talking about what we do with our heart and passion allows others to understand and connect. Better than that, we can invite others to engage with our business and buy from us. To do this, we start with the inspiration and know the client journey and then allow and help them to take that journey.

When we stand in our truth and get out of our own way, we can truly make this about our clients and allow them to engage with us and our business.

> **ACTION:** Write a few lines about how you first felt about starting your business. Why did you start your business? What ignited your passion and got you to take that leap?

## Less Machinery, More Humanity.

When people first meet me, they say they have been taught all the sales tricks and tactics, and none of them work. I agree. Let me tell you why.

The machinery of sales (the tactics and strategies) is essential. But what is more important is to put that machinery to use in a way that benefits humanity. Too often, we (badly) employ the tactics we have learned and then blame the tactics. We use the machinery of sales without connecting it to the human we are speaking to and then wonder why it doesn't work.

We do this because we fear sales, being ourselves, and being rejected. We hide our humanity behind the tactics. When we choose to do that, we are stopping people from connecting with us and stopping the flow of opportunity that may arise from the connection.

> **ACTION:** Please forget all the sales tactics you have ever learned. Don't try to use them. Just try to connect, be open, and allow the conversation to happen. When you see an opportunity to ask more questions – do that. When you see an opportunity where you can help someone – offer that.

## Less Cleverness, More Kindness and Gentleness.

When talking to prospective clients, we think that what we are supposed to do or what they want to see is how clever we are, how we have mastered our art, and how we are perfect. We act cleverly. We talk about ourselves and our achievements. We talk up everything.

The truth is that all people want to be heard and understood. They want to know that you understand who they are, what they are trying to achieve, and their problems. We must be gentle, listen, and probe to get people to share this information. Only once we understand the other person should we engage and think about talking about ourselves and what we do.

Prospective clients want to know, above all else, if we can help them and that only happens when we first understand where they are and what they want to do and not do. More than that, they want to get to know and believe in us, which only happens when we are transparent and authentic. To be more authentic, we must be kind and gentle with ourselves and expose our mistakes and wins. We must be honest about how we approach and work with our clients.

> **ACTION:** Think about what questions you should be asking your prospective clients to learn more about them, and then share some stories you can share about where you made a mistake and what you learned from that.

In the next chapter, we dive deep into listening. If you think you know how to really listen, think again. I know you will learn something new and important if you keep reading.

CHAPTER 11

# Are You Really Listening?

> Some people without brains do an awful lot of talking, don't you think?
>
> — SCARECROW, *THE WIZARD OF OZ.*

Everybody listens – right? Wrong! Everybody can hear, but not everybody listens.

This chapter is about teaching you the key points of being a better listener. This will help you get the most out of your meetings with prospective clients. And may even save your marriage (or other relationship).

Listening is essential because if you are going to help your client, you have to listen and understand what their problems are. You are also listening to how they feel and what motivates them so you can help them make a great decision. You can only do this if you fully understand what they want and, more importantly, what they will say yes to.

You are also listening for 'fit'. Fit with you, your business and your solution. Sometimes, from listening, it will be clear that this person is not your client — and that is ok.

You need to be able to answer this question:

> "What are the things that are important to this person that they will want to take action on?"

Typically, important problems or areas come in three categories:

1. Business-based — for the whole business
2. Team-based — for that team
3. Personally based — what's important and a driver for the individual.

If you show prospective clients that you can help them achieve their goals in all three areas, they will say yes.

Good listening uses all your senses. This chapter examines what that means and how you can use all your senses to improve your listening skills.

## What Is Listening?

Listening means that you are concentrating on what the other person is saying. When people think about listening, they start with words — but a University of California study showed that words only make up 7% of communication. Most information (55%) is gleaned from body language and eye contact, and the remaining 38% from vocal inferences such as tone, pitch and speed.

This originates from the work of Albert Mehrabian, a professor at the University of California, Los Angeles (UCLA). It is often referred to as the "7-38-55 rule[8].

Once we have "heard" the words and taken in the other information, we decipher and interpret this through our brain. Each person's brain employs filters. These have been built through our life experiences, and we use these filters to help us decode what we hear and experience.

Have you ever witnessed a conversation and then found you had a completely different interpretation of what was said? This is an example of personal filters at work.

## Using Your Body to Listen.

### The Ears.

Let's start with the most prominent part of your body. Listening involves your ears. When you listen, you hear the words that someone says and their tone, speed, and other inferences that help you interpret what they are saying.

According to Kay Lindahl, author of *The Sacred Art of Listening: Forty Reflections for Cultivating a Spiritual Practice*, you may not know that we spend only 45% of our time listening. Even when listening, we are distracted, preoccupied, or forgetful about 75% of the time[9]. Interestingly, she also notes that, even immediately after listening to someone talk, we usually recall only about half of what we said.

**Improving your listening effectiveness.**

- Put yourself in a position in the meeting room or café that will give you the least distractions.
- Sit opposite the person you are meeting so you can hear what they are saying and have a good vantage point to see their non-verbal communication.
- Be quiet and ready to listen.

## The Eyes.

You know when someone is listening because their eyes are engaged with you. You look at their eyes or mouth and see what their body language tells you. Breaking eye contact disrupts your connection. If you need to write something down, ask permission, write it down, and check in with the other person that you have noted it down correctly. Sometimes, it is easier to write notes after your meeting so you can note all the things you experienced and heard and what the next steps are.

Knowing yourself can help when you are listening. For example, I find it hard to concentrate when there are other visual distractions, such as people walking past or television. Knowing this, I choose to sit in a position that minimises this distraction.

As stated earlier in this chapter, body language makes up 55% of communication, so knowing some fundamental body language indicators can be helpful. However, there are cultural differences, and body language can easily be misinterpreted. Be sure to check with the person to ensure that you understand their actions correctly.

I watch for body language when reviewing my proposal with a potential new client. If you observe, you can tell when they are following your words. If I see that I may have lost them, I stop and check-in. This allows them to ask questions and lets me know they understand what I have said so far in the meeting.

Here are examples of how I might approach this:

> *"How are we going so far? Do you have any questions or things to clarify?"*

> *"Oh – I seem to have lost you on that point. Let's stop. Do you have any questions?"*

Understanding all the nuances of body language is an art. I have read and heard much from Allan Pease and would recommend his material.

## The Body.

Our body gives others a lot of clues about how we are feeling and what we might be thinking. If you want your client to be open, use your body to show that. Standing or sitting in an open position, with arms uncrossed, smiling, and looking at them, will help you to listen with all your senses and send a positive message to your client. Open body language, confirming with your gestures and spoken affirmations, will tell the other person that you are genuinely engaged in active listening.

Mirroring is something that all humans do naturally when we are engaged in active listening. Copying their gestures and body language is a technique that will help put the other person at ease. Try leaning your head the same way or crossing your legs to copy them. You can also use this to do the opposite. For example, if you are talking with someone and they have their arms crossed, you can more visibly open your arms to try to get them to open up.

Next time you are conversing with someone, watch for things that happen during the meeting and how they impact how you listen and feel about the other person.

Here are some examples:

- Finishing each other's sentences
- Interrupting each other
- Filling in pauses in the conversation
- Looking at watches/phones

- Sighing or frowning
- Reading something from a piece of paper.

The best way to improve your body language is to be conscious of what you do and what helps you listen more actively.

## The Brain.

We speak to be listened to and have our ideas validated. Actively listening and being present validate the speaker even when the listener does not say or do anything.

We assume that listening is a matter of exposing ourselves to what others say and that this is listening. Honest communication happens when one person transmits a message, and the other receives and responds. Listening happens in the interaction between people.

Listening is a social interaction; what we hear is filtered and interpreted based on our knowledge and experiences. That is why listening can be done without sounds or words. We interpret silence, gestures, and body movements. Have you ever seen a ballet dancer? Their movements speak volumes.

When we actively listen, our brain interprets the information from all our senses. Listening and interpretation can be practised as you become more aware of what your different senses tell you and how you combine the various ideas to conclude.

## The Mouth.

The whole point of practising active listening is to accurately understand what you have heard and seen and match this to what the other person is trying to convey. You know what has been said once you have listened with all your senses and allowed your brain to interpret. Your mouth can be used in listening to share with the other person what you have understood and check that you have interpreted what they are trying to communicate correctly. This is often an iterative process, particularly with complex or emotive ideas, until both parties agree that there is a joint understanding.

To do this, ask questions, but don't interrupt. Use your questions to clarify when there is a break in the conversation. Ask questions to gain a deeper understanding and allow the other person to elaborate on what they are discussing with you. Asking questions shows you are interested, listening and focused on gaining the correct interpretation.

## Getting Ready to Listen.

1. Take a deep breath to get centred.
2. Clear your mind and give your full attention to the other person.
3. Be aware of any self-talk, distractions, and assumptions you may have, and try to let go of them, at least temporarily.
4. Listen with all your senses, paying close attention to the other person's tone and nonverbal communication.
5. Be silent until the person finishes speaking.

# Distractions to Listening.

Often, we are so busy thinking about other things or what we will say that we forget to truly listen. These internal and external distractions mean that we either don't hear all the words and see all the nuances or don't interpret them correctly.

**Improving your listening:**

Here are some tips on improving your listening:

- Have an intent to fully listen when you approach the meeting.
- Have specific goals for each meeting to find information to help you present a solution to this client.
- Remove distractions such as exterior noises, mobile phones, etc.
- Stop thinking about what you want to say about things unrelated to the topic.
- Sit opposite the person and up straight so that you are in the best position to see all non-verbal cues.

- Sit intending to listen and have a notepad ready to write down important points.
- Get into the habit of summarising and repeating what you think you have heard to ensure you have it right.

Don't let "things" get in the way of your ability to listen.

- Remove your phone and other devices from the table and ensure they are switched on silent and won't disturb your concentration.
- Prepare a pen and paper with the business's name, date and who you are meeting before you go in.
- Don't be tempted to pick up the pen and doodle or play with it if you are a fidget.

## What Are You Saying?

The world's best business communicators have strong body language and a commanding presence that reflects confidence, competence, and charisma.

Here are some tips about conveying optimism and confidence:
- Hold your body upright and point your torso and feet at the person you are listening to.
- Tilt your head to one side to show you are listening intently.
- Look at the person you are talking to.
- If you are addressing more than one person, take turns focusing on each person while speaking.

- I try to focus on the person most interested in what I am saying.
- Also, make sure you focus on and notice the body language of the decision-maker.

> **Sales Tip:**
>
> If I am addressing a finance point, I look at the person most likely to be interested in that topic.
>
> But make sure that the others around the table understand and are on board before progressing.

Doing all this while listening, watching, interpreting and talking about your business takes preparation and practice. The more you do it, the less conscious you will be about each element, as they become second nature.

Give yourself time and space. It is tiring when you first learn something. As you become a better listener, this process will become easier and less tiring.

People who speak with confidence use their hands to explain a point. Think about using your body to give meaning to what you are saying.

## Further Ideas to Explore

How we think and feel about ourselves in a given moment is written all over our bodies. The people we speak to and meet in our day pick up on this information subconsciously or consciously.

• • •

Here is a thought-provoking and powerful TED Talk by Amy Cuddy called *Your Body Shapes Who You Are*:

https://www.ted.com/talks/amy_cuddy_your_body_language_may_shape_who_you_are?language=en

• • •

Watch some great speakers in action. I love TED.com. Find a topic here you are interested in and see how the speaker engages with the audience. Here are some of my favourites:

https://www.ted.com/talks/sir_ken_robinson_do_schools_kill_creativity?

https://www.ted.com/talks/simon_sinek_how_great_leaders_inspire_action?

• • •

Do you know what you look like when you are in action?

Videoing yourself and reviewing later gives you the best chance to see this, but if that isn't feasible, try sitting or standing in front of a mirror to see what you might look like to the other person. Or ask colleagues that you are taking to the meeting to give you a critique.

## What Are You Listening For?

Listening is about words and so much more. Here is your **real** guide on what you should listen for and why.

You will know that you have listened well if you understand what the person wants and why they are motivated to do something about that.

**What problem do they have?**

Problems have lots of dimensions. Once the person you are speaking with has opened up about the problem, your job is to DIG and ensure you know the full dimensions of the problem. Here are a few ideas:

- When did it start?
- What have they tried?
    - What was successful about that?
    - Why didn't it work?
- Who is affected by this problem?
- What would a solution mean to the business, the person, and the team?
- What would success look like?

**Look out for the emotions!**

Listening to and observing someone speak about their business and particular problems is a wonderful opportunity to understand the emotional and logical reasoning behind the problem. If you can understand what motivates the need to change and address this problem, then you will be much better equipped to influence decision-making. When you fully understand the elements that have contributed to this problem in the first place, you are in a better space to speak to those when it's your turn to speak.

**Is there politics?**

Listening will also help you understand how decisions are made in this business and the role of the particular person. Here are some questions to think about on this:

- Who do they need authority from to make this decision?
- Are decisions made in an autocratic or inclusive manner?
- How new and secure is this person in their position?
- Are there other players who need to have their ideas included and concerns addressed?

If you understand this, you can formulate a solution that includes some answers to these internal issues.

**Phrases:**

Where possible, I like to listen for particular words or phrases that I can use when describing the solution to them. In this way, I can create the message of a more complete "fit" between our solution and their business need.

People feel heard and seen if we can accurately show them that we have listened by describing them and their problems.

In the end, your listening will enable you to understand the other person and fit your solution so that they understand it logically and emotionally. Lastly, it allows you to create a solution that all parties agree will work.

## The Power of Silence.

When we question what makes a great salesperson, very often, one of the first things people say is, "*The gift of the gab!*" My answer to this is, "Well, yes and no". Yes, it helps to be able to speak to people. But I would contend that there is more profound power in silence. Let's explore why and how.

### Silence says you are confident.

If you can be silent in a conversation, ask a question, STOP, and LISTEN, this sends a powerful message to the other person. Silence says you are comfortable in your skin and confident with what you are and stand for.

### Silence allows others to think and speak.

If you are going to influence someone, you need to understand deeply what they think and feel about a topic. By using silence in our conversations, we **allow** the other person to stop and think about what we have said and our questions. It will enable them to think clearly about what they want to say before they say it. The outcome is often a much clearer and deeper answer. This allows you to understand better and craft your proposal more precisely to meet your client's needs.

## Speaking After Silence Has Power

Don't be afraid of silence. Take your time; when you are ready to speak and pitch your idea to the potential client, it will have more clarity, and your client will appreciate the effort you put into putting that together. Sometimes, speaking too quickly sounds like an "off the shelf" pitch, making the client feel "sold at".

The bottom line on silence is this. We are all different. And if you are naturally quieter, I encourage you to be that way. You are like this for a reason. For those of you, like me, who know how to talk (and talk), there is real power in having light and shade in your presentations and being quiet and listening when required.

There are times for talking and times for silence. I encourage you to experiment with both and see how each makes you feel and their impact on others.

Take your time and allow the power of silence to work for you and your client.

You can learn to improve listening, but staying on top of it takes concentration and constant work, like any discipline.

Part of listening is asking great questions and understanding your client deeply. That's what we will be looking at in Chapter 12.

CHAPTER 12

# Meetings, Questions and Finding a Fit

"Never question the truth of what you fail to understand, for the world is filled with wonders."

— L. FRANK BAUM

Our tongue is one of the most potent parts of our body. Use it wisely!

Before we talk about using your tongue, let's think about the purpose of our sales meeting. We are there to investigate, understand, seek and help. We are exploring with our client to help us understand their problem more and then, if it works, to see if there is a fit between their problem and our solution.

Your first sales meeting is a powerful opportunity to understand more about your clients and get them to see if your solution is an excellent fit for them. This hinges on how you use your tongue and the questions that you choose to ask. Curiosity and wonder are great tools and will be essential in your endeavour to understand more about your client.

Meeting Structure is one of the main problems I help people who want to improve their business meetings. Once you have the right structure that focuses on the client, the ensuing conversation will help move them on their buying journey. And with some practice, this will flow. You feel more comfortable in these conversations, creating a more efficient, effective process and more paying clients.

Remember, your client is Dorothy – she is new to this world. Our goal is to understand what she wants and help her know the journey that we are asking her to embark upon will help her gain an answer to what she wants.

## Before Your Meeting

Do your homework! Prospective clients will love that you have tried to learn more about them. Review what you know about the client. This should include who referred them to you (if applicable) or how you found them, as well as information about their business from their website and a more general search from LinkedIn and Google. Review Chapter 9 for more on this.

## Arriving

Be early – you don't want to be flustered and late for your meeting! Take your business card, pen, and notepad with you.

Your first goal is to learn as much as you can about the target business and the person you are meeting with. When waiting in the foyer – have a look at any awards and other information that is displayed. Even what is and isn't there will tell you something about the character of the business. I always like to pick up a copy of their newsletter or the like, as this will tell you about their communication style and interaction with others.

I remember one first meeting that I had, whilst waiting in reception, where I saw some art – a painting by Howard Arkley (a famous Australian artist) – on the wall. I walked up to have a closer look. It was an original! This observation allowed me to start a conversation with the business owner about how there was an original Arkley in a small suburban office!

Your first meeting is an excellent opportunity to get to know your client. Look for clues to tell you more about the person you are talking to. Here are some suggestions:

- Where is the office located?
- What type of reception area is there?
- What are they wearing?
- How do they greet you?

You are looking for clues to understand better how this person approaches their business life. In the first 1-2 minutes of the meeting, you should have some answers to these questions:

1. Are they formal or informal in their dress/office/delivery?
2. What is the environment like in their office?

3. Do they have a structured or unstructured approach?
4. What other interests do they have?
5. How comfortable are they in meeting with you?

## Introductions

From the first moment, your goal is to make your potential clients feel at ease and show them that you are interested in them. Smile and show that you are friendly and interested. Use open body language (arms open, palms facing them). Your goal is to open the conversation and get them talking about themselves and their business as soon as possible.

## Your Sales Meeting Structure.

This is **your** meeting, so take charge (nicely). Your client expects you to do this, guide them through the questions you need answered, and explore potential solutions. Remember, selling is a dance. You are asking them to dance, and so it makes sense that you lead. Here's how.

### Beginning

The beginning of the meeting is all about building rapport. This is an essential ingredient for the rest of the meeting, and it also helps you and the other person feel comfortable. Once they are relaxed, they will open up and give you fuller answers that will help you understand them and their needs better.

## Take Control of the Meeting

- It's up to you to have an opening question, the icebreaker. Since you have done some research on this person, let's use that! But don't make it too bold.
- Let the client know how you work with clients using a Client Roadmap (see Chapter 7). This puts the meeting in the context of the larger sales agenda.
- Set out the goals for the meeting – both for your client (by asking) and for you (by sharing).

Once you've established the goals, the beginning of the meeting will be complete. At this point, I like to ask permission to move forward to the next step by saying, *"Great, we've got our objectives out on the table. Is it okay if we move forward now?"*

## Middle of the Meeting

In the middle of the meeting, you focus on building **trust and credibility** (see Chapter 5). People buy from people they like and trust. The best way to do this is to ask lots of questions so that you uncover precisely what this person's problem is and all the details around that problem.

Remember, people buy emotionally, so start with the logical structures of their problem and ask questions about the impact on them, their team, and their business. Most importantly, ask them how this makes them **feel**. There is more on how to use your questions later in the chapter.

Think about some things you can take with you, such as some physical evidence like case studies, reports, or other material that will help build your **credibility** concerning what you're talking to this client about. These can be used after your questions.

Remember that later in the meeting, you will dream with your client; these tools may be beneficial. More on this later in this chapter.

## The End of the Meeting

The first thing to do is to thank them and to check that both of you have met the expectations from the start of the meeting. If you have missed something, this is the time to cover that, or if you are out of time, organise how you will do that.

Summarise the meeting to show that you've listened to them and understood their pain and their issues. It's also good to recap on the solution you've dreamt up with your client and, lastly, mention the things you need to go away and check on. This shows that you're being open, honest and transparent with them.

## Organise Your Next Step.

While you've got the person in the room, ensure you get a commitment for a date and a time for the next steps. That might be a phone call, or it might be the presentation of your proposal. This step is **vital** because it ensures you are committed to working towards your next interaction with the client.

At the end of the meeting, the last thing to do is make sure you're clear about the actions you and the client will take to progress the sales relationship.

Smile, thank them and part on a personal note.

### Back in the Office

**Follow up email.**

When you return to the office, email all of the elements from the end of the meeting – the thank you, the summary, and the next steps – so that the client understands that you've heard and listened to them today. Make sure the next steps are in your diary and that you deliver!

## Questions, Questions, Questions.

> "Successful people ask better questions, and as a result, they get better answers."
> 
> —TONY ROBBINS

Right at the beginning of this book, I told you that selling was about helping other people buy, helping them on a decision-making journey to make an excellent decision for them and their business.

People will buy from you when they:

1. Have a problem they want to solve.
2. Believe that you can help them solve that problem.
3. Are ready to solve the problem.

The problem not only needs to exist – but it needs to be in the top three priorities for this client right now. We all have limited time and resources to address issues or to go after our aspirations. So, understanding this problem and its importance to your client is an essential step.

Have you ever talked with a friend about a problem and understood more about how you were feeling and what you were thinking? When we are close to a problem, we don't always see it in its complete or accurate light. Part of what we are doing in asking questions is helping our clients think through and understand their problems.

We are also helping to map out the logical, tactical, and emotional pointers that have brought this client here. The second part is arguably more important.

Just like Dorothy – they are here for a reason. They are, in part, running away from home (because it's not fair), having been through a storm and landing somewhere strange and interesting. Our questions help them explore how they got here and where they are now. This new landscape will help them gain insights into their business and grow self-awareness.

## Why Questions Are Important.

### Let's Dig Into What You Are Trying to Uncover With Your Questions.

Your first job is to understand the problem and why it exists in this business. Think of yourself as an investigative journalist. Your job is to ask lots of questions, to get the client talking, and to uncover the logical, tactical, and emotional reasons that this problem has been created or uncovered. You are discovering what they want to tell you and what they are reticent to express or unaware of.

As you build out these questions, your clients will tell you more so that you can better understand their needs and wants. You are helping not only find the right solution to their problem, but more importantly, you are helping them explore their problem from a new outsider's perspective.

As you go through this process with them, and they start to appreciate the insights, this will create loyalty and trust. Because you have helped them in this endeavour, they are more likely to want to do business with you, so they will be less open to speaking with your opposition and less price-sensitive.

## Where to Start With Questions.

I like to start with questions I already know the answers to or questions I know will be answered with a "yes". These are typically close-ended questions.

There are two key reasons that I do this. Firstly, I want to feel my way and start with questions I am comfortable with, which I know the client will answer easily and positively. The other reason is that they are more likely to continue once people have started saying yes. Try this with your kids!

Your goal here is to create comfort for you and your client. You will start seeing your client open up and relax, allowing you to explore more.

### Opening Exploration Questions.

Here are some examples:

- Can you tell me a little about your business?
- What are the top priorities for your business right now?
- Use current events (that are business-related) and then ask them to say how their business is finding that or responding to these events.

### Questions to Build Your Understanding.

As the late, great Stephen Covey said: *"Seek first to understand, then to be understood.*[10]*"* I know you remember that **Great Selling** is about helping the other person make a great buying decision – for them. If our premise is to help, we first must understand our client, their business, and their likes and dislikes (to name a few).

The other thing we are doing here is collecting the facts and building blocks. These questions are easy for your client to answer and build your understanding based on what they say and how they say it.

1. Tell me a little more about your business.
2. Can you tell me about your organisational structure?
    a. How many employees?
    b. How many offices?
    c. Geographic structure?
    d. Vertical structure (around industries or products)?
3. What is your position within the business?
    a. What are your main KPIs?
    b. What do you enjoy about your job?
    c. What's the hardest thing about your job?
    d. What would you like to change?
4. Why do clients buy from you?
    a. What's your competitive edge?
5. Can you tell me how your business makes decisions about _____?
    a. Who is involved?
    b. What's the typical process/number of meetings?

Once you have gone through these "easy" questions, you can introduce other ideas and questions that help you go deeper into the problem.

# Questions That Get Down to the Real Problem.

Once you know more about the business and the person, your next job is to identify the problem(s) your client wants to do something about.

Typically, people want to do something about the things that drive economic value. They are:

- Increasing revenue
- Reducing costs
- Reducing risk.

There is a saying often quoted (and attributed to) Warren Buffett.

> "Price is what you pay. Value is what you get."

In this part of our questioning, we discover what our client values. If we know where they place value, we can better show how our solution fits in with those. This is important because we want our clients to **get** what they value. Why? Because that is what they believe they are paying for.

This quote initially came from Benjamin Graham, the author of *The Intelligent Investor*.

Quantify what revenue or cost impact this means for your client.

- How much does it affect revenue/costs?
- How often does this happen?
- How long has this been happening?

- Is this an increasing problem?
- What's the impact on:
    - The business
    - Their job
    - Them personally?

Don't forget to ask them how they feel about these things. Everyone makes buying decisions emotionally and then wraps the logic around it. If you only get the "economic factors" and not the "personal factors", you only have half the story.

## Qualifying Questions.

Qualify the business impact of the core problem — help them dig into the problem and uncover all aspects. Here are some questions to try:

- What have they tried in the past?
    - Who was involved?
    - What worked?
    - What didn't work and why?
- Where to from here with this problem? What's your next step?
- If you could fix this, what would that mean for:
    - You
    - Your job
    - Your business?
- If this isn't fixed, what would that mean for:
    - You
    - Your job
    - Your business?

## Feelings, Nothing More Than Feelings.

Remember, we are looking for the logic and how this makes them feel. When you get close to these areas, give them space to talk. The best way to do this is to stay quiet. Let them explore their feelings and encourage them with nods and affirming noises.

Try something small and simple if you need to prod them with words.

> *"You mentioned _____. Can you share a little more?"*

> *"When you talked about _____, I could see that this means a lot to you. Can you help me understand this better?"*

Don't be afraid of emotions and feelings. They are a natural part of both life and business. If you can be comfortable with these and ask these questions, you will help your client do the same. This will build intimacy, which is the strongest determinant for building trust.

When people trust you, what they will share with you is quite remarkable.

## Getting the Client to Dream and Help Build the Solution.

Once you're comfortable with understanding the problem, the next thing is to get the client thinking about what a great solution might look like. The word "solution" helps uncover the rational things.

- What does the solution look like for them, their department, their business, and their clients?
- Who else does this problem impact, and what does a good solution look like for them?

I also use "success" because "What does success look like?" has a different impact, and you're more likely to get some emotional answers to that question.

One of the things that you're trying to uncover here is what a great solution is, including delivery. What does the team who's going to deliver it look like? What help might they need internally to deliver this successfully?

## Finding the Fit.

You know the problem, and you've worked on a potential solution with the client. If you see a fit, now is the time to explore that. I don't give you permission here to start talking about you.

Here are some examples of questions that help with fit:

> *"So, if we could provide a solution that looked like this <explanation>, what would that mean for you?"* and listen.

> *"So, if we were going to try and implement that type of solution, who might be involved in that implementation?"* and listen.

> "Who are the people deciding this, and what's important to those people?"

Get more information once you have found some items you can help with.

I like to use straightforward questions here, like:

> "You mentioned _____ – can you tell me more about that?"

You want to find out about:

- The costs associated with the problem.
- Staff time wasted.
- Is this a priority for their superiors?
- What ideas have been tried to remedy this problem to date?
  - How have they worked?
  - What could have been done differently?

## Talk a Little About Your Solution.

Do this only at the very end and use it to summarise what you have learned. For example:

> "We have a _____ that addresses _____ concern that you have. It does that by _____ and _____. The next step would be for me to go and put together some more information about how _____ can specifically address your needs."

## Questions That Need to Be Answered by the End of the First Meeting.

You are there to help your client in their buying journey. So, remember there are pointers on the Yellow Brick Road that will help them (and you) understand the parameters they need to make a buying decision.

Here they are:

1. Know if they have a budget assigned to address this problem.
    a. If you can find out what it is.
    b. If they don't have a budget per se, gain an understanding from them that there is a commitment from the business to spend money on this.
2. What timeframe is assigned to this budget (this financial year, etc)?
    a. Do you have an implementation date in mind?
3. What is the buying process for your client?
    a. Who is involved in this?
    b. How long does this usually take?
4. What criteria will be used in the decision-making process?
    a. Who is involved in this?
    b. Who else are they talking to?
5. Typically, this will involve one or more of these:
    a. Product or service features and benefits
    b. Product quality
    c. Professional support or ease of use
    d. Investment
    e. Image.
6. Know the next step and the timeframe.

A quick check that you know the answers to:

- Who is buying (influencers, approvers, decision makers)?
- Why are they buying (stated reasons (logical) as well as often unstated (emotional / ego, etc)?
- What are they buying (hopefully your products and services)?
- How are they buying (what is their preferred process plus, of course, the money question)?

## Great Questions for the End of the First Meeting

*"If there was a solution to _____ problem that we have talked about today, what would an ideal solution look like for you?"*

*"If there was a solution to _____ problem that we have talked about today, what would an ideal solution look like for your business?"*

*"If there was a solution to _____ problem that we have talked about today, what would an ideal solution look like for your boss?"*

## Make Sure You Do This Before You Leave.

- Say, thank you.
- Sum up actions and next steps.
  - Do this for all the people in the meeting.
  - Include who is responsible and when the next step will be done.
- Set the next phone call/meeting (time and date).

I cannot stress enough the importance of having the next timings set. When you send them a proposal or make that follow-up call, it makes it much easier if you have set the day and time for this.

Reliability is something that builds trust. If you leave a meeting without specifying **when** you will have the next piece of information (e.g. a proposal) to the client, you are opening yourself up to being seen as unreliable. It sounds unfair. But here's how it plays out. When someone hears that you will send them a proposal, and you don't specify the timing, then they make it up. They will think they will have it this week, next week or in a month. They will see you as unreliable if you cannot meet the schedule (that is in their head).

Here is what that sounds like:

> *"Thank you so much for the meeting today. As I mentioned, my next step is to prepare a proposal based on our discussion today. I will have that to you by close of business on Thursday."*
>
> *"Given that I do that, when should I call you again?"*

Set a day and time. And then confirm that back to them.

This is so important! Picking up the phone to talk to them on that day and time will feel easier for you. You will sound more comfortable and confident. Confidence sells. Just like people want to eat in restaurants with people already there, your clients want to buy from someone confident in their solution and themselves.

•●•

But wait – there's more! When you set a date and time with someone, they feel more compelled to pick up the phone. They have committed to do this.

You will spend less time wondering when the right time to call is. You will be more confident when you call and are much more likely to get through. This all adds to your sales efficiency, and let's face it, running a business doesn't leave you with a lot of spare time!

## What to Do Once You've Left That First Meeting.

Take some time to stop and summarise your thoughts on:

1. What went well/not so well?
2. What have you found out about the problem and the person?
3. What next steps have you confirmed with the client?

Make sure you follow up with an email that:

1. Thanks them for their time and sharing their thoughts on _____ problem/idea.
2. Confirms the next steps:
    a. From them
    b. From you.
3. Confirms your next point of contact with them.

Invite them to call you should any questions come up in the meantime.

When you have done this well, you will leave Dorothy to start on the Yellow Brick Road. You will have some ideas on what she is likely to encounter and how you might help her as she does that.

In our next chapter, we look at what a proposal should look like. This is one of the BIGGEST mistakes I see people make, and it is so easy to fix!

CHAPTER 13

# Proposals Are About Your Client – Not You!

> "It's not where you go or what you do, it's who you take along that makes the difference."
>
> — L. FRANK BAUM

One of the biggest problems in proposals is that people are fixated on talking about themselves! You know, one of those people who are constantly on about themselves. Typically, their conversation ends with: *"That's enough about me. What do you think about me?"*

Before you read any further, grab a proposal you have prepared for a client. If it starts with About Us, Why Buy From Us, or Clients Who Love Us (or anything similar), this chapter is for you.

Nobody likes talking to people who only talk about themselves. Nobody likes reading proposals that talk about you and not about them and their problem. As humans, we want to be seen and understood. We want to know that other people understand us and our problems and want to help us in our lives and businesses.

There are three key things that your client wants to know from you in your proposal:

1. Did you listen to them, and can you repeat this to them so they know you understand their business?
2. Can you show that you understand their problem?
3. Can you show them you can credibly and reliably help them with their problem?

Before we delve into "how" we write proposals, let's start with the "why".

## Why Do You Write Proposals?

You write proposals to win clients. Simple! It makes sense then that your proposal should be tailored to persuade your potential client that you are the best business to help them solve their problem. Keep this at the top of your mind as you read on.

One of the biggest mistakes that people make is to have a laundry list of their achievements. It's a bit like trying to talk to someone, and all they do is talk about themselves. It's a turn-off in conversations, and it's a turn-off in proposals.

Your proposal isn't about you. The central character in your proposal is your client. You only have a role in this movie if you can show that you can help them be the star of the movie who gets what they want.

# How to Write Proposals.

Follow these proposal tips, and I promise your clients will be happier to read your proposal, AND you will win more business.

 **Build a Proposal That Your Client Can Relate To.**

You need to show them that you understand them, their business, and their particular situation. This can be done by summarising what you have learned from your meetings with them.

There are also some subtle ways that you can show your client-orientation through a written proposal:

- Feature their logo on the front and each page of the proposal.
- Make their name and the name of the project bigger than yours.
- Use their terminology and words where possible.
- Show that you have done extra research and taken care to get things right:
  - use their mission statement or other material from their website
  - use the correct spelling for the names of the people, their titles and, of course, the business.

This summary of the client and their current problem typically takes 1–2 paragraphs or up to a page.

Remember to be kind in what you write about them. Sandwich your description of the problem with what they are doing that is great or steps they have already made to develop their business and work on this problem. You don't want to fill them with dread by only giving them bad news.

They already know that they have this problem, so you are showing them that they are seen and understood.

### Step Two: Build a Proposal That Helps You Tell Their Story.

Your proposal should follow the same logical steps you addressed during your meeting(s) with the client. In your first meeting, you started by asking them to help you understand their business and then working through the problem that you are there to help them with.

As you build out the proposal, and as it follows the same pattern as your meeting, the client will feel comfortable. They feel this way because they are reading their story. They are reading what you have already discussed and covered together.

The proposal tells the story not only of the problem but also of the solution that you have already canvassed with them. Familiar, plausible, and building each step consistently allows the reader to know that you understand and then begin to recognise that there is a solution to their problem. It shows them that this might be something that can move them forward.

They want to believe in you – but more than that, they want to believe in themselves. They have worked hard to build a business, department or team. They want recognition for this and to know that the tricky bits are hard for a reason and that there is a way through.

You are building a story to take them down the Yellow Brick Road, to invite them to continue, even when things get tough. If you think about how Glinda did this, it was all about showing Dorothy that she could find her way home. By travelling along the Yellow Brick Road and seeing the wizard, she would find the answer to her problem.

 **Step Three — Build the Solution — Remember WIIFM (What's In It For Me).**

Building a solution should now help the client follow that Yellow Brick Road. But remember to keep the central character, well, central!

What's In It For Me (WIIFM) is the **only** radio station people listen to. Our brains would literally explode if we couldn't tune in and out of messages and information. We filter everything as part of being human. Your client is no different.

Yes, they want to know that you are credible and reliable. But more importantly, they want to know that you know them intimately and can show them something that speaks to their unique problem.

Their problem may be similar to lots of others that you have solved. Your client wants to know this as it builds your credibility to help them. But, and it's a big but, your client also thinks that their version of the problem is unique; their problem has nuances you can see and address.

In my meetings with clients, whilst I look for similarities with other clients I have worked with and problems I have solved, I am also looking for their unique elements. Once you have built your credibility about solving this for others, you must also identify their differences.

This helps you stay on your toes (and not go into auto-solve) and helps the client uncover what is going on for them and why this problem exists. All with your help.

Focus on the benefits your client will get from using your product and service. You can apply this in a proposal format by stating the feature and then relating the specific benefit of this feature to the client's needs and how it addresses their problem.

Remember to make it real for them. Don't use generic examples. Use examples from their business with names, places and problems that are real to them.

My favourite way to check with myself that I have done this well is to finish this sentence:

*... and what this means to you is ...*

Here is an example I love to use when coaching my clients.

**Feature:** My car is red.
**Benefit:** We all know that red cars go faster.
**Value:** And what this means to me is that I will never be late for school pickup.

When I am presenting the proposal, I know I have done this well because there are lots of nods and smiles as the person recognises themselves in the proposal.

A great way to summarise your solution is to have a roadmap. Clear steps that the client takes to overcome their problem. We want this part to be credible and for the client to read themselves into the movie as the star.

If you have made assumptions or have questions that need to be clarified, put those here so that you can go over those with your client before looking at the investment component. You can use this to discuss the investment and next steps.

### Step Four: Why Should They Do This? What's the Return on Investment?

During your meetings and discussions, you have put together an understanding of why this client should do this right now. When writing a proposal, you repeat the story you uncovered together. This component is essential to quantify the benefits for those reading the proposal.

This is important because we ask them to buy from us after reading this proposal. We need to validate and quantify the benefits. By including a summary of our discussions, you are helping to make this process as simple as possible.

The return on investment component has two components.

**1. Hard benefits.**

The hard benefits are measured in dollars:

- Increased revenue
- Reduced costs
- Reduced risk (and potential cost of not reducing that risk).

In this section, if you can, you need to show that their investment in your solution can be paid off in a number of months based on the benefits you have calculated.

If there are no direct benefits (from increased revenue or reduced costs), then the risks (and their potential costs) must be explored in more detail.

**2. Soft benefits.**

Many proposals don't include soft benefits. But they are important. I include them because many things I have discussed with the client don't directly impact the dollar. They are, however, important.

Remember, you never know who will read this proposal and their decision-making style and preferences, so it's always worth spelling out all the benefits you have uncovered.

**3. Be clear about the investment required.**

Before I launch into the investment required, I like to focus on the Return on Investment (ROI). Remember in Chapter 12 when we ask many questions about what happens if this problem is and isn't solved? Well, this is where that comes into play in your proposal.

The ROI component is, arguably, more important than the investment. If we can build a case that makes this a "no-brainer"; that builds a return that makes it virtually impossible for them to say no. Build this return equation from their words, using their numbers and the insights you gained from understanding their business and problem.

The ROI isn't only about money. You also need to spell out the softer benefits and ways that this will improve their business and situation.

Remember to consider what the client may need to invest (other than money). How much staff time will be involved, or what information will they need to provide for the project to proceed smoothly?

Make the proposal's investment component clear and concise, so there are no hidden costs or items to surprise your client later.

### 4. Getting to yes.

Your job is to help your clients have all the correct information so they can make sound business decisions in a timely manner. If you can demonstrate this consistently, your client will say yes!

Repetition is your friend. It helps people feel comfortable and heard. This is just as true for you. Consistency is a part of our psychology — we admire consistent people. In Robert Cialdini's book *Influence, the Psychology of Persuasion*, he describes why this is and how this works (Cialdini, 2021, p. 303)[11]. When building our proposal or asking questions, we can start with things that the person will agree with. Things we already know the answer to be "Yes".

If we have written a paragraph or two and the client thinks, "Wow, this person really listened to me and is describing this really well," the reader will be much more forgiving when working on the areas we know less about. They want you to be consistent.

You can use the proposal to run your presentation meeting with the client. You should treat this yes in the same way as any other. What I mean by that is that this is just the next step in having a supremely happy client. Be clear about what people must do next and when, to keep the ball rolling.

## Don't Give Them Too Much Information!

A salesperson's primary job is to give the prospect the **right type** and **amount** of information to get them to say yes to moving forward with the proposal. Getting a no is equally as good. Remember that **Great Selling** is about making the process efficient and human and not about the outcome. Yes and no are equally as good.

Does your proposal have to be correct? Yes! Does it have to be precise? No! I know that sounds a little strange. So, let me explain.

I know that to some people, this idea sounds manipulative and a version of lying. It's true; some salespeople use this technique for these purposes. But bear with me; there is a method in my madness. Let me explain to you why and how this sales technique works.

The profession of sales is about giving the client the right amount of information to answer their questions and convince them that the product or service will indeed fix their problem or meet their need. To do this, you need to know about your potential client and what problem they are interested in solving. Done properly, this is about helping them buy, not manipulating them into something they don't want.

I have intuitively done this in my sales career, and I was fascinated to happen upon a *Harvard Business Review* article by Bob Frisch called "To Get Better Decisions, Get a Little Fuzzy"[12]. It asserts that if we focus too much on precision, this wastes time and money. It goes on to say that allowing some imprecision leads to better decision-making.

When you are selling to someone, it can be just like this. If you are getting buying signals (nodding of the head, them talking about implementation plans (for more, see Chapter 16)), then it is time to start moving on to looking at exploring the signup process with the client. Do they know everything about you, your product, your business? No! But clearly, they have heard enough to start thinking about the next step.

As you know, we are nearing the end of this book. And if you take nothing else away from reading this, then know this: Your job in **Great Selling** is facilitating the buyer's buying process. Giving too much information can stop them from helping themselves.

Have you heard the term "analysis paralysis" (or when too much information stops the whole decision-making process)? The idea of the "Paradox of Choice" was first published by psychologist Barry Schwartz in his book *The Paradox of Choice: Why More is Less*. He made consistent findings that, while increases in choice can give better results, there is a law of diminishing returns. He also noted that, at some point, this leads to greater anxiety, indecision, analysis paralysis, and dissatisfaction[13].

Sometimes, when we are presented with too much information, this can produce anxiety and fear. So, can I suggest you put less in your proposal than more? The process is about your clients, so be guided by them. Some people will want more information, and if that is the case with this client, then find out what they need and provide that. However, don't think this means all clients will want this.

By now, you know I love movies! This reminds me of *The Sound of Music*. Maria starts with a stream of *Do Re Mi*. She realises that she has lost the kids, and then she breaks it down to help them understand. So, "Let's start at the very beginning"!(Wise, 1965)[14]

The next chapter examines the sales process and the results you must focus on.

CHAPTER 14

# Reframing Your Results for Great Selling

"You had the power all along, my dear." Glinda, the Good Witch of the North

— L. FRANK BAUM, *THE WONDERFUL WIZARD OF OZ*

## Sales Greatness.

Greatness isn't about you. **Great Selling** isn't about you. **Sales greatness is evidenced by what we see when we help others to produce or create.**

One of the key reasons that people **hate** selling is because they view it as, or are scared to be seen as, manipulative. The easiest way to change this is to change your approach. It sounds simple, and it is.

When you approach a prospective client, don't think you are trying to sell them something. Your first and most important job is to get to know them and to see if there is a problem that you can help them solve. **Great Selling** is about helping people buy things that solve their problems.

We need to carry this intention and mindset throughout the whole sales process. The journey is theirs, not yours. At each step, we look at how we can help this client move towards a decision for them, not for you. You will see patterns in these decisions as you get to know your clients. These patterns will reveal topics, tools, and stories that will help you ease their way and make the journey easier, perhaps quicker, and more reliable.

This is why it is critical to focus on your ideal client and the problems you solve in their marketplace. Great business and **Great Selling** are about knowing your "fit" with your client and their problem and aspirations. This knowledge helps you be more confident in approaching your potential clients. It also gives them confidence in you.

Confidence sells. The other way of saying this is that clients want to work with people who can confidently talk about who they are, what they do and how they can help them. If you can easily talk about helping other clients with the same problems and experiences, they witness someone who knows about their problem and has solved it for others. Now that's a sales centrepiece. That story will attract and take people on their problem-solving journey.

The thing about attitude is – you get to choose your mental approach! You are in charge! And remember, your attitude (and its attractiveness, or otherwise) is judged by the potential clients you meet, not by your ego. Here are some quick checks.

**Do:**

- Know what problem you solve for your clients.
- Know who your ideal client is.
- Practice having confident conversations with others about these things.
- Make sure your attitude is positive before you set out to practice.
- Go out and talk to people and find what makes them tick.

**Don't:**

- Assume the other person isn't interested in you. (They are interested in solving their problem, and if they don't have the problem – they aren't your client).
- Talk about yourself. Your first job is to find out about the other person.
- Give up. **Great Selling** is about practising and improving with each attempt.

## Glinda, the Witch of Sales Goodness.

Glinda, the Good Witch of the North, is my favourite character in *The Wizard of Oz*. She knows so much, yet she allows Dorothy to go on her own journey so she can discover it for and about herself. **Selling is very much the same.** It is not our job to tell others what to do, merely to suggest solutions to their problem, give them a credible pathway, and be there to support their journey. The decision to take that journey is theirs. I want to explore how you can achieve more Sales Goodness.

## Sales Goodness: Let's Start With You.

As you will already know from reading this book, my reader probably feels uncomfortable selling, even though they know this is important in their business. I know that sometimes you enter a sales meeting or call feeling like Dorothy – a fish out of water. But **you are Glinda** to your clients and potential clients. You have so much knowledge and understanding; all you need to do is share that Sales Goodness lovingly and carefully with your clients. We forget that our knowledge and experience, which seems mundane to us, is impressive to others. It's time to start sharing.

The best way to do this is to start with understanding your Dorothy, understanding what storm and circumstances have brought her here. How can you introduce her to Oz and describe the Yellow Brick Road in a way that helps her know if this is a good fit for her?

Your Yellow Brick Road, or at least this starting version, is just the first steps and an idea of what is at the end. It definitely shouldn't have every step people take. Give your Dorothy a clear place to start, a path to follow and a destination. Their discovery along the way is theirs. We are there to help them start, not to take the journey for them. When we allow our clients to go through their journey, we help them make better decisions.

It's like when your kids are learning to tie their shoelaces. Yes, you can tie them for them each time. But you know that this means they will never learn for themselves. Eventually, you stop doing it and start coaching and cajoling them. Even when you know, this means they will be late for school and you for your meeting. The journey is theirs to discover, find their confidence, make mistakes, and pick up the pieces. But they don't have to be alone.

## Sales Goodness: Allow Your Clients Their Sales Journey.

Glinda knew very well that Dorothy had everything she needed to go home – simply by clicking the heels together on her ruby slippers. Instead, she allowed Dorothy to go on a journey of discovery – where she found that she had the brain, the heart and the courage (and the slippers) all along. In the journey, Dorothy also learned how to sell and help others find their needs. She realised that she had compassion, empathy, strength and intelligence. All the traits that a turning point, a rite of passage, needs for success.

Yes, there were fields of opium and flying monkeys and a witch who wanted her dead. But these were for Dorothy to discover at the right time.

We know so much about what we do, but the clients' journey matters. The beauty is that we discover new things if we allow and observe. Allow them the journey. Allow yourself to learn new things about this journey as you see each new client through it. There are so many riches in these stories. They, indeed, are where the gold lies.

> "I'm glad I don't know everything, Dorothy, and that there still are things in both nature and in wit for me to marvel at."
>
> — L. FRANK BAUM, *GLINDA OF OZ*

## Sales Goodness: A Mature Relationship.

Selling is about establishing a mature relationship. Your client must trust you enough to tell you what they think and feel. You must honour this valuable information and trust and only use it for good. You can use this information to persuade and suggest things that might be able to help them on their journey. But in the end, you allow them the space to make their decision and take their path.

Sometimes, the people we are talking to choose not to go down our Yellow Brick Road. We show our pathway with love and allow people to choose. It is okay; all is still good in the world.

A mature relationship isn't fixated on "Yes". It isn't about getting to yes; it's about allowing people their journey and being there if you are the one they choose. Let them be them, and let you be you.

There are enough great sales relationships to fill your bucket and then some.

I remember a beautiful story that I once heard about imperfection. It goes like this:

*There are two water pots.*

*Each day, a man takes up both pots and walks down to the river to fill up the pots with clean water.*

*Each day, the man takes these full pots back to his home. The thing is, one of the pots has a crack in it. It loses water each day on the trip back.*

*This makes the cracked pot sad. He wants to do a better job for his owner.*

*One day, the sad, cracked pot gets up the courage to ask his owner why he doesn't get him mended so he can do a better job.*

*The owner laughs, a kind laugh. He tells the sad, cracked pot to watch on their trip back, and he will explain.*

*On their trip back, the owner slows down and talks to the sad, cracked pot. "Can you see all these beautiful flowers that edge your side of the path?"*

*"Yes," says the cracked pot.*

*"Well, these flowers are here because you help them with a little water from our walk home. These flowers brighten my day and lighten my load. They bring me joy!"*

Our cracks aren't imperfections. They are ways of brightening someone's day. It's okay to be who we are and not know everything. The joy, my friend, is in the journey, the water we dedicate to that journey, and the flowers that grow from this.

## Sales Goodness: What Glinda Did.

Here is how Glinda used Sales Goodness with Dorothy. She:

- Addressed Dorothy's fears.
- Helped her feel comfortable, where she was at.
- Allowed her to understand where she was (the starting point).
- Suggested a credible pathway for her to take.
- Told her what might be at the end of that journey.

## Sales Goodness: What Glinda Didn't Do.

- Tell her everything that was along the way.
- Interfere – unless it was life and death.

I wish for you to choose to be good and true in your journey and that in your sales, you allow others the space to be good and true, too. Sales Goodness isn't about winning or losing or about greatness. It's about helping someone solve a problem in a way that makes them more knowledgeable, capable and a better person.

> **Glinda:** For the record, I knew you had it in you all along.
> **Oz:** Greatness?
> **Glinda:** No. Better than that. Goodness.
> — L. FRANK BAUM, *THE WONDERFUL WIZARD OF OZ*

## Objections Are Your Friend, Not Your Foe.

Often, people that I coach are fearful of objections, of being rejected, of the "No". OK, I get it. But this only stings when we are only focused on "Yes". Instead, when we are focused on helping others and have enough potential clients in our pipeline, then a "No" is great news because it means you can lovingly leave this person, for now, and move on to others who are still on the journey.

Here's another way to take the sting out of objections. In buying psychology, an objection means that people are thinking about buying from you. They see a hurdle and want to know how you can help them overcome it. It is part of their buying process. I am more frightened of clients with no objections, which tells me they may not be serious about considering my offer. If you can help this person overcome their objections, they might just buy from you. So, love them and lovingly take your client through their questions and concerns.

There are two kinds of objections. First are the logical, straightforward questions people ask about buying or using your product or service. Most of these are easily dealt with. People's hidden fears strike fear into the unwary seller's heart.

The truth is that people will assume that you are aware of their objections, and so have the answers for them. Or they will think it is your job to coax it out of them. This is where I wholeheartedly agree. It is your job.

Once you know that someone has an objection, you have a chance to explore the reasons behind it, and once you understand, you can effectively answer and overcome the objection and keep following the Yellow Brick Road.

## Why Objections Exist.

Before I go into how I want to explain why objections exist, all objections, in one way or another, relate to a fear that the client has. Fear is not rational, and so often, the first objection that is explored is not the real one because you have to pass the test of answering it successfully to get to the "real" issue.

Remember, this is part of our client's journey. We want to find the objections and help our client answer them.

## How to Listen to and Answer Objections.

**Listen to the objection.** Let your client take their time so that you understand precisely what's bothering them. Look at how they sit to pick up valuable clues from how a prospect says and phrases their objection.

**Ask some questions.** Make sure you really understand what this means for the business, your client and others that this decision may impact.

**Confirm it with your client.** Once you are sure you have a handle on this, state your understanding of the problem to them.

> *"What I have heard is that you are concerned about _____"*

This gives them a chance to clarify further if needed.

**Explore.** Once you have the first reason, explore. Often, this isn't the real underlying concern. Your client may not want to tell you the real reason first (as it is often personal and emotionally based). Explore more for the implications of this:

> *"You mentioned _____. Can you tell me how you have experienced that problem in the past? What has it meant for you / your team / your business?"*

**Answer the objection.** You understand the objection. Now you can answer it. But remember, what they are really talking about is fear; your job is to answer the logical question AND address the underlying fear. Again, stories about other clients and how they overcame the same objection are perfect here. Need help? Look at the Feel, Felt, Found stories in Chapter 5.

**Are they satisfied?** Have you answered their objection? Are there other areas that need exploration?

Rinse and repeat.

## Confidence Is Everything and Nothing.

Let's face it: sales is about confidence! To be the salesperson for your business, you must build your confidence in yourself and your business. Once you have done that, you can show confidence in your business, what you do and how you do it. That's **Great Selling**.

Here are some ideas for building sales confidence:

### It's All About Attitude.

If you feel awkward about selling it will show. Stop thinking about sales as selling and start thinking about it as helping people buy. That's what great salespeople do.

### Don't Be Desperate!

People buy when **they** want to. This happens when you convince them of the benefits they will receive when using your product or service. It's then that they are happy to spend their money with you.

### Know That You Are an Expert in Your Business.

One of the things that experts are happy to do is to **talk about what they know**. Once you understand what the client is looking for, then as the expert, think about how you can help them **solve their problem** or fulfil their need.

## Are You Feeling Low in Confidence?

Want to know what I do if I'm not feeling the self-love? I get out of the office and **talk to my clients**. They are the best at helping me realise my positive impact on their businesses. Can't get out of the office? No problem. Just pick up the phone!

We all have our own way of rebuilding our confidence, so I encourage you to find yours. But know this: selling is an active sport played in front of clients. In some ways, you can **only** get your sales confidence by playing the real game with a real client.

## Build a Self-Confidence Routine.

I got this tip from Susan Ward, a course presenter in small business promotion[15]. A self-confidence routine is a great idea. If you are going out to represent your business, think about these ideas:

- Choose to **wear an outfit** that helps you feel confident.
- **Be prepared** by doing your homework on the topic and client.
- **Visualise** having a great conversation or meeting with them.

## It's All in the Words You Use.

Do you **sound convincing** when you speak? Next time you are on the phone or at a meeting, record yourself and listen to how you sound.

Here are some **power sales phrases** that might help you:

**Change** "If you want to discuss the benefits ... "
**To** "Let's discuss how the _____ will benefit you."

**Change** "I hope you find this interesting ... "
**To** "I am sure that you will find this of interest."

**Change** "It might be a good idea to meet ... "
**To** "Let's meet next week to discuss this further. What day suits you?"

**Great Selling is all about having fun** with what you do and the people you talk to. Don't forget to **reward yourself** when you do a fabulous job, and keep handy copies of the **wonderful things people have said about you** to pep you up when you need it.

My last word of sales advice is, just like I say to my 14-month-old girl when she falls over, pick yourself up, dust yourself off and **try again!**

CHAPTER 15

# Asking Doesn't Need to Feel Yuck!

"No thief, however skillful, can rob one of knowledge, and that is why knowledge is the best and safest treasure to acquire."

— L. FRANK BAUM, *THE LOST PRINCESS OF OZ*

## The Truth Is Simple!

Whilst it may be true that others cannot rob us of knowledge, we can sometimes shroud ourselves from our knowledge and our truth. Fear clouds our brains and pushes us to choose things that don't make sense. This chapter is about rethinking and reworking your brain with some simple truths.

In **Great Selling**, there are some simple truths – truths which I have laid out in this book. As you have been reading and taking in new ways of thinking and doing sales, I hope you now understand the simple truth — that people "hate" or fear selling because some people sell the wrong way. Their "bad" thinking leads to "bad" actions, which lead to bad outcomes for all parties. Everyone is worse off.

This is why we distrust selling and salespeople, squirm at the thought of selling or being a salesperson and why businesses and people fail in their endeavours.

The truth is simple to understand. The truth is difficult to execute continuously.

## This Is the Truth:

- **Selling isn't** something that you **do to** others.
- **Selling isn't pushy** and isn't about convincing others to buy from you.
- **Selling isn't** about **talking first** and getting your message across.

This is Crocodile Selling, and just like I wrote at the beginning of this book, just because we can see crocodiles (people who sell in this way), it doesn't mean that we are in the age of the dinosaurs. Their time is done!

## Great Selling Is …

Selling is a walk, a journey, that you take with your clients. It is an invitation for them to take a journey with you. It is a journey of discovery. They will agree to do this if you can show them honestly how you can help them with a pain or need. Sometimes, they decide to walk with you; sometimes, they answer no. The journey is built around their buying and decision-making process. It is your job as a salesperson and businessperson to guide and help them.

We can do that because we have travelled this path many times. We are experts in our field and guiding others in this decision-making journey.

**Great Selling** is about understanding others, where they are, and helping them on their journey. The results of this journey can be many and varied. Clients journey with us for a long or short time. Sometimes, their journey takes them to work with others or empowers them to continue independently. All of these outcomes are okay because we are helping them on their journey, which sometimes means we must let them go.

In helping them decide to buy (or not to buy), our role is to understand what they need. Which pieces of information they need, and in which order? Different clients have different needs, so stopping and understanding what is important for these clients right now helps them to know and make the buying decisions that they believe are good for them.

**Great Selling** is about listening first. We cannot hope to help others unless we have listened and understood. You can only help your clients once you know something about them, their needs and desires. You can only help them once you have listened and understood.

Chapter 11 is about listening better, so if you haven't read this one yet or want a refresher – maybe it's time to have another look.

This chapter is about helping you understand this honest pathway – this journey of **Great Selling.**

## To Be Great Is to Have Courage.

> "You have plenty of courage, I am sure," answered Oz. "All you need is confidence in yourself. There is no living thing that is not afraid when it faces danger. The true courage is in facing danger when you are afraid, and that kind of courage you have in plenty."
> — L. FRANK BAUM, THE WONDERFUL WIZARD OF OZ

To be fearful is to be human. It is how we choose to describe and react to that feeling that lives in our gut, the feeling that makes the difference in how we both perceive and respond to a situation.

I was listening to the radio recently, and a researcher was talking about reactions to fear. They had worked with two people. The fear of public speaking paralysed one, and the other was an extremely successful international performer. What interested me (and the researcher) was that when they described how it felt in their body and the physiological symptoms before they performed or spoke, their descriptions of what was happening in their bodies were almost identical. The difference lay in how they perceived that energy and those symptoms. The names they used for this were paralysis, fear, anxiety, excitement, or anticipation. This naming then also ultimately impacted what they chose to do with their experience.

If it is true that our bodies show us the same reaction, then we have the power to channel that "nervous" energy and rename it anticipation. This reframing will help us feel better about our body's response, act differently, create better interactions with clients, and ultimately gain more clients. How great is that!

I have experimented with this idea on myself, my clients, and my children. I've helped them reframe their words to describe their physiological symptoms. It is wonderful to see that a-ha moment on their faces.

In writing this book, I have done some further research on this and have found some affirming research from Alison Wood Brooks from Harvard Business School, who writes:

> *"I expect that reappraising anxiety as excitement, compared with reappraising anxiety as calmness, is easier and improves performance on important tasks that typically make people very anxious."* (Brooks, 2013).[16]

## Are You a Lion or a Mouse?

As you might remember, the Lion felt like he could jump out and growl at Toto because Toto was small. The Lion thought that he could scare a little dog. So, he was acting more like a mouse than a lion.

I was coaching a client the other day on precisely that. I was helping her work out an approach to speaking with new clients. She asked, "Shouldn't we start with the ones that I don't think will say yes, the ones that I'm not interested in"?

The answer: No!

Two reasons:

- If you are calling someone you don't want as a client, you aren't really invested in the call. This will impact what you say and how you come across in the call or meeting.
- The whole point of talking to potential clients is that you want to grow your business. You don't want to grow your business with clients you don't want. Let's instead grow with clients you LOVE and who LOVE you. Don't waste your energy and time improving skills for people who don't fit that story.

Even though you can practise many skills, like running, our bodies must focus on different areas if we run the 100m versus cross-country. Hone the skills you want to use with clients you want to work with.

As the Wizard said,

> "The true courage is in facing danger when you are afraid, and that kind of courage you have in plenty".
> — L. FRANK BAUM, *THE WONDERFUL WIZARD OF OZ*

## There Are Two Things I Know About Selling.

**Thing One — You Are Enough.**

You already know how to sell and speak to people. Engage with them and get them to buy from you. The one thing standing in your way is YOU and how you react to the feeling in your gut. You don't have to be anyone else other than you. People prefer you to be authentic.

### BE YOURSELF

**Thing Two — Practice.**

The only way to learn how to sell is to get out there and do it. Yes, you will have wins. Yes, you will have failures. It is through the journey, the experience, and the practice that you will learn about yourself, your clients and the process that brings these together. You will find your sales courage.

Get out there, my friend. Stop being a pussy cat and lion up!

# GET OVER YOURSELF.

These are my two great rules for selling.

1. Be yourself
2. Get over yourself

## How to Ask for the Sale.

In Chapter 12, we looked at asking better questions. This focused on how to ask better questions to help the client (and you) better understand the problem they wanted to solve, which you may be able to help them with.

One of the reasons that we get so anxious about "asking" is that we think about this as being the end of the sale, the opportunity for people to say "yes" or "no".

Let's change how we think about that. Instead of focusing on the end of the process, I want you to practise your "ask" muscle throughout.

Here are some examples of asking within the process:

- When you ask someone if they want to know more after a new introduction.
- Asking for a meeting to learn more about the client and their problem.
- Getting permission to ask more questions.
- Seeing if they would like a proposal.

- Figuring out with them what will work in the play out of the solution so that you can write that story into your proposal.
- Asking for a time and date when you will speak again.

All of these micro-asks help you to build your sales courage. They allow you to test the waters and get permission for the next step in your client's journey. If we focus on their process and asking along the way, the final "big" ask suddenly isn't that big anymore. You are used to asking and helping the client answer.

This is the sales dance.

Each ask and answer helps you learn more about your clients and their wants. A great dancer works with their partner so that you both look great on the dance floor. So, whilst doing the same dance with each client, each one will be slightly different as you expertly manoeuvre with each client on **their** dance.

## Signposting Your Dance.

When you ask someone to dance, you probably say what style of dance you will do – do you want to waltz is a very different question to do you want to tango! This allows your client to make an informed decision about whether they want to dance (or not).

This is what I call signposting. It is a great way to get micro-permissions along your way, too. Remember that in Chapter 7, we talked about your Sales Roadmap. This is a physical version of your sales journey that you can use to help you overcome your nerves and graciously signpost to your client.

Here is what this sounds like:

> "Thank you so much for meeting with me today. I want to ask you some questions to better understand your business and the problem you are keen to solve.
>
> Once we have done that, if there is something I think I might be able to help you with, I would like to discuss that with you and flesh out what that might look like for you and your business.
>
> Finally, if we find something we both think will work, we can discuss the next steps and what works best for you around timing and implementation.
>
> At the end of the meeting, we will have the framework for a solution, allowing me to assemble a proposal for you.
>
> How does that sound?"

This is so powerful because it relaxes you. After all, you have laid out all the steps on the table, and now all you have to do is walk with them down the Yellow Brick Road. It also allows your client to relax. They know what is happening and what sort of dance you are asking them to join you in.

As you practice and become familiar with this dance and you leading it, I promise these words will flow. I know from coaching my clients that often they start thinking, "*I could never do that*", and then there is something that clicks in their heads, and they say things to me like, "*I can't believe I started to sound just like you – the words came easily and felt natural.*"

## Sales Etiquette for Following Up.

Following up is probably the sales activity that most people (salespeople and non-salespeople alike) struggle with. Either they don't do it or do it poorly. It goes into the too-hard basket, resulting in clients not being helped and money on the table!

### Why People Don't Follow Up:

It all comes down to how you "feel". People don't follow up on their sales calls because they don't plan a time and date for this with the client. They don't get permission from the client. Because of this, they feel like they are intruding, and the person doesn't want them to call.

You know the things that go through your head.

- It's too soon. They probably aren't ready to talk yet.
- It's too late. They have probably forgotten about me.
- If they wanted it, they would have called me.

It is also because we are frightened of getting a "No".

I want you to know that there are yeses, nos and maybes in **Great Selling**. All of these answers are great answers. Our job in

**Great Selling** is to help them make a good decision for them. It isn't only focused on yes; that makes the sale about you and not them. That is where the ickiness of Crocodile Selling comes to bite you.

**Great Selling** focuses on the process and not the outcome. When you have a great process, you will get great outcomes.

## Why Follow Up?

Ok, truth time. **In sales, it is YOUR JOB to call the client.** I want you not just to imagine but also to know that your client doesn't have any numbers on their phone. They can only receive calls. They can't call you! Pick up your phone and give them a call because they are waiting for you!

Selling is about listening and helping. If you have listened, worked with and explained how you can help them with a problem they want to solve, **then they want you to call**. You have asked them if they want help, and they have said, "Yes". It is now up to you to follow them through this journey.

Your client doesn't call you because, just like you, they get busy. They put you on the to-do list but don't get around to it. Even if they know it's a priority for their business, there is a reason they have been avoiding doing something about it. You need to help them help themselves.

When you call them and get them "back on track" with something important to them, they will not think you are pushy or annoying. They will appreciate your dedication to their problem. They will like it.

Using the dance analogy, imagine that you have asked someone to dance, and then, with the music still going – you stop – and walk away. They expect you to lead the sale, so please do it.

Like learning to dance, I will share some great ways to make this smooth, gracious, and not icky and pushy.

## How to Follow Up.

**In the meeting:**

When you are in a meeting (or phone call), it is your job to ensure that you **always** have the time and date for the next step(s) organised at the end of that interaction.

Here is an example of how to do this:

> *"Ms Client, thanks so much for your time today. We have discussed (summarise their main problem and how you can help). You have asked me to (summarise action points). I should be able to get this done by (give a date). I would like to schedule another time to see you (or call) to answer any questions and discuss the next steps."*

**When you are organising the time with the client, make sure to:**

- Get their **permission**: *"Would it be okay if I called you on Tuesday morning?"*
- Set the **time and date** (if possible).
- Note it down and put it in your **diary**.
- **Send a thank you email** summarising what you have learned, how you can help and the next steps, including the date and time of the follow-up you have organised.
- If you have organised a new meeting time, offer to **send a calendar invitation** so you know it is in their diary. They'll appreciate it because you are saving them time!

**What if they say they will call you?**

**Don't panic!** It's always best for you to have a next step, even if they say this.

Often, they say this because they must discuss things with someone else or just want some breathing space. Here's an example of what I say:

> *"No problem. When do you think you will be able to get back to me?"*

They give you an answer.

> *"Would it be okay if I haven't heard from you by the following week, I give you a call?"*

Ninety-nine per cent of the time, people will say **yes!**

This works for you because when they have permitted you to call, you will! **It's that simple.** Better than that, when you go to call them, you **feel** better about the call. This is an appointment that you have agreed with them to have. This "feeling" gives you confidence, and confidence sells. You ask better questions, listen better, and speak more eloquently. These are recipes for better client connections, leading to more sales and better client relationships.

When we call and feel confident, we tend to sit up straighter and feel better. This is important because it changes the timbre of our voice. Try it for yourself. Sit crouched on your seat and feel like you are invading someone's privacy. Then, hear what your voice sounds like. Now, imagine you have a ruler up your back and a smile on your face. Your voice changes. This is important because, in communication, only 7% of understanding comes from your words and 38% from how you speak. Your client infers things from your pace, tone and timbre (Mehrabian, 1971[17]). This is one reason why some people prefer to do their sales calls standing up.

This also works for your client because they have told you they want you to call and expect to hear from you. The other thing I learned from using this technique, particularly for introverted clients, is that they are likelier to answer your call. Why? Because they have permitted you, they feel obligated to do so.

For both of you, though, it stops you from wasting time trying to connect. It allows them to let you know about other things that are going on (such as meetings or holidays), so you aren't wasting your time calling when they aren't in the office.

So now you know why you need to call, let's step through what that might sound like.

### The Call:

**Strategy for call:** Remember the structure: You, Me and The Next Step

**You = talking about them.**

> "Hi Bob, I'm calling as we discussed in our meeting.
>
> I remember from our meeting you were keen to ... (add points here)
>
> I think the proposal stepped that out for you.
>
> I'm curious: what are your thoughts on the proposal."

Your aim here is to get them talking. Talking about the proposal, and more importantly, if any changes are needed to make it "fit" them better. This can also help you better understand their buying process. Who did they discuss it with, and what insights did they learn? This should take the majority of the phone call.

**Me = How you can help them do what they want.**

> So Bob, what I've heard you say is ... (Repeat back the main points)
>
> How we would do that is ... (What are the next actions?)
>
> Do you think that will work?
>
> Is there anything else we need to work on together?

**The Next Step = What's the next step in their buying process?**

> "So, the next step from here is to ...
>
> How does that sound?
>
> Great ... I will <list next steps>
>
> Looking forward to speaking with you again soon."

**If you get Voicemail:**

First, don't panic. This doesn't mean they don't like you anymore. My first thought is that they are busy and probably in a meeting.

Here's the type of thing to say:

> "Sorry, you couldn't make our 10 am call. I know that sometimes meetings run over, so I will give you another call in 15 minutes. Speak then."

## Second Call:

Use the same format as above.

### Second Voicemail:

> "Sorry, I missed you again. I know that days and appointments can go awry. I am going to do two things. Firstly, I will give you another call (pick a time in the afternoon.) Secondly, I will email you some suggested times so we can tee up something that works for both of us."

### Third Voicemail:

> "Sorry that we keep missing each other. I will send you the email I mentioned to find the next best time to connect."

## Send an email:

Send an email to organise another time to call.

Give them two options that work for you.

Then end the email with this:

> "If neither of these times suit you, can you please help me by letting me know a time that works for you, and I will call you then."

## How Many Times Do You Call?

I would leave 6–7 voicemails and send a couple of emails.

Really? Yes! The fortune is in the follow-up. To be honest with you, this can be many more when your whole job is selling.

So go with how you feel and what you think. There will be a time when you feel it is fruitless to continue when you have given it your best shot.

## The Last Call:

I call this message the Goodbye Message. This is the call that ends the follow-up series.

> "Hi Bob, I just wanted to leave you one last voicemail.
>
> I wanted to say thank you for your time and for considering our services. I really enjoyed learning more about you and your business. I know we get busy and can only focus our time on the problems and solutions that are a priority in our business right now, and I totally understand that.
>
> I wanted to let you know that this is the end of my Follow-Up Calls, and I will send you one last email.
>
> Thank you again, and wishing you all the best in your business. If there is something we can help you with in the future, please don't hesitate to get in touch."

Let me unpack what is happening here.

1. You are letting them off the hook. They probably feel bad that they haven't returned your calls, so releasing them is right.
2. From this — two things will happen:
    a. You won't hear anything — in which case you were right — they have other priorities.
    b. They will call soon — because they **want** to be on the hook. And this will give you a chance to reconnect and get back on track.

Either way, both of you feel better about ending it in an adult way. And if they want your help in the future, you have left that door open so they can call you.

The other great thing about this is that it allows you to stop. Put a neat bow on the top of this box and move on. Remember, **Great Selling** is all about the process, which needs to feel great for you and your clients.

Like in life, this journey of selling and learning about yourself and your clients never stops. With each step you take, you will learn more, apply what you have learned, and develop new skills.

That's why — you never stop selling, which is our next and last chapter.

CHAPTER 16

# You Never Stop Selling

Life and business are both a journey. Like in life, you never stop living and learning; the same is true for your business journey and selling. As you evolve in your business, you change. Your ideas change, your clients grow and change, and even what you give your clients changes. It makes sense to keep talking to your clients about these things as you learn and change.

I think of it a little like gardening. Once you have harvested the crops, you dig in the remains of the old crop, invest in the soil, and start over again. The subsequent crop benefits from the previous one as it supplies nutrients to the soil. The worms ingest the old crop as the foliage breaks down, creating a natural fertiliser.

If your business is your garden, we also need to weed it. Sometimes, the weeds are toxic clients; sometimes, the weeds can come from our hubris and mistakes. Either way, we need to clear them out.

In Chapter 14, I wrote about Glinda, the Good Witch of the North and how she shows us how to have a mature relationship with our clients. A mature relationship doesn't just happen; it doesn't maintain itself once we have established that with our client. We must develop and grow our client relationships and the skills that foster them.

We know that sometimes our internal "flying monkeys" need to be tamed and that sometimes our clients walk off the Yellow Brick Road into a field of opium poppies – and fall asleep and just forget. Either way, our clients need us to be honest and true in our dealings. That's how we continue to help them, to be of value.

## Showing Your Clients Love.

I am using this theme to show how **you** can improve the sales in your business by loving people more. Improving sales to me means:

- Ensuring your current clients feel loved so they are happy and referral-ready.
- Selling new things to clients that they love.
- Meeting potential new clients whom you can show love to.
- Converting those potential clients into clients who love you … go back to the top, and repeat.

## How to Show Your Clients Love!

**Get to know them.**

How well do you really know your client? This may sound like a silly question, but there is a method in my madness. People share personal things with those they **like and trust**. They are happy to share things that are going on in their lives: the good, the bad and the ugly.

Chapter 5 shows that people buy from people they **like and trus**t. It follows that when they share personal information with you, they like and trust you – so they are likelier to buy from you!

Have you ever met someone that you think is PERFECT? Never a hair, word or anything out of place. I celebrate them, but how likely are you to tell them something you stuffed up, a mistake you made? *Not very, right?*

The truth is none of us is perfect. But, for some reason, we think this is what other people want to see. People relate much better to you **if you are YOU**. Honest, open and authentic about all the wondrous, funny, gritty and down-right revolting things that happen to you in life and business. More on this a bit later.

**Show you are there to help.**

Now you are out showing everyone how much you love them – let's add some business **substance** to this. If you love your clients with businesses, add a quarterly (six monthly or annual) visit (or phone call). I prefer a visit because you learn so much more about their business from seeing it in action. In this visit, use these ideas:

- **Share with them** what you have been working on and learned since you last spoke.
- **Share with them** what you are looking forward to in the next period.
- **Ask them** what they have been working on and learned since you last spoke.
- **Ask them** what they are looking forward to in the next period.
  - **SEE** where you can help.
  - **ASK** if you can help.
  - **THANK** them for their business.
  - **ASK** for a referral to someone else you would be able to help.

Love isn't just about the sale!

Showing love to your clients isn't just about the sale or business. Here are some ideas on how you can show clients love:

- **Send them** a birthday card and gift related to your business (voucher for your business).
- **Send them** something to say thank you.
- **Send them** something about things that are important to them (Golf, Movies, Cycling, etc.).
- Use your newsletter to **share information** on what:
  - You are doing, learning, and looking forward to.
  - Your clients are doing, learning and looking forward to.

Love is also about asking questions and being open to the response from your client.

- Ask your clients **what they want**, where they are having trouble, and/or where they are seeing opportunities.
  - **SEE** where you can help.
  - **ASK** if you can help.
  - **THANK** them for their business.
  - **ASK** for a referral to someone else you would be able to help.

In sales, you never stop learning, listening or asking.

## Honesty and Mistakes.

Mistakes happen. We are human. You know it, and so does your client. It often perplexes me why people avoid talking about mistakes with their clients.

I call it – dead cats on the table. Everyone knows that they are there. Let's get them up on the table and talk about them.

If you can take the front foot when mistakes happen, they can help build stronger relationships with your clients. These positive sales stories can help others understand more about you and your business. This shows them how you act when tricky things happen.

That might sound counterintuitive, **but it isn't. Let me tell you how this sales technique works.**

**Everyone in the world makes mistakes.** There is something "too glossy" about a person or a business who doesn't own up to their mistakes.

People and businesses are often loathe to be honest. I think this is because they are scared to show "weakness" and fallibility. Curiously, the opposite is true. Brene Brown wrote in her book "Daring Greatly" that vulnerability is instead our most accurate measure of courage ([18]Brown, 2012).

When we choose to be vulnerable, we choose to be authentic. This sharing of our reality encourages others to do the same. It shows our honesty and courage and that we are in this relationship with our client for the long-haul. I have had many instances where we have made a big fat mess with a client, and by owning up, working it through and fixing the mess, we have improved our connection and relationship.

### Let's Take It a Step Further.

Perhaps your business is used to fessing up to individual clients, but I would like you to take it a step further. **I want you to use your mistakes when speaking with new clients.**

Again, this might seem counterintuitive, but I want you to think about it in the reverse. If someone trying to establish a business relationship with you tells you about their mistakes, what does this tell you about them?

Here are the messages that I know come from telling the Sales Stories of your mistakes:

**You are honest.**

It shows that when mistakes happen, you take responsibility for them and work it through, even to the point that you are happy to talk to potential clients about what happened.

**You respect your clients.**

It shows that you have the respect to be open and honest about your mistakes, what you did next, and the outcomes. Respect and honesty are easy when times are good. This illustrates how you show respect when the going gets tough.

**It shows your process around mistakes.**

It shows your prospective client how you deal with mistakes when they happen, as we all know they will in the future. This encourages your client to trust you. If they need to use it, they know how to approach you and how you might respond.

**It shows you are a learning organisation.**

My friend Einstein says that insanity is doing the same thing over and over and expecting a different result. The most important element that telling the stories of your mistakes shows to others is that you learn and change when you make a mistake. You put things in place that change your business to avoid this mistake or deal with it differently.

Your clients aren't stupid. They know that you make mistakes. They want to know how you deal with your clients and the repercussions. They also want to know how you review your business and change so that less mistakes happen.

In my experience, these stories are well received by clients and have built trust in me and my business.

## Practical Ways of Talking About Mistakes.

We've all had things go wrong. It is how we choose to deal with these that is important. My first advice is to do this face-to-face wherever possible. From a relationship perspective, you must take the time, but more importantly, people are less angry and irrational when you meet them face-to-face. It also allows you to read body language and understand more than just what their words are saying.

Before you go in, have the intention to be honest and transparent. Ensure you have done your homework to clarify what happened and how you want the conversation to go. Remember, just like all sales conversations, you must take the lead.

Sometimes, this is the very time we know this client isn't right for us. That's ok, but end it nicely.

# Mistake Telling Structure.

**Show them the Yellow Brick Road.**

Taking charge in the meeting isn't about making it all about you. It is about flagging how this discussion is going to progress. Something like:

> *"Thank you for meeting with me today. I know our mistake has been difficult for both of us. What I would like to do is:*
>
> 1. *Go over the history of how we got here.*
> 2. *Talk about what happened.*
> 3. *Talk about the next steps and where to go from here.*
>
> *How does that sound?"*

**Start at the Very Beginning ... a very good place to start.**

By the beginning, I mean the first time you met the client. Why did they come to you, and what did they want to achieve by doing that? Particularly, if you have had a long history with the client, it helps to reaffirm the good you have done during your time together.

**Where it went wrong.**

This is where you detail the circumstances around the problem, why it happened, and take responsibility. The critical point here is to ensure you know and show that you have investigated the root cause of the issue and are happy to share what you know.

We all know that sometimes, there is more than one finger in the pie. This is your chance to be honest about that, too. When you apportion blame, ask it a question rather than make a statement. Use phrases like *"my understanding is ..."* and *"... wondering if you can help me understand what happened from your perspective ...".*

When talking about responsibilities on the clients' side, find a way to ask about those gently. Here are some phrases that might help:

> *"It's really important to me to understand what happened from your side.*
>
> *From what I have been able to find out ...*
>
> *Can you tell me a little about that?"*

This part of the story aims to start a conversation with the client, explore your understanding of what happened, and expand this with new information from the client. This isn't about blame or having the client think you are not taking responsibility. This is a conversation, not a confession. The aim is to get a complete picture so you can both move forward.

**Moving forward.**

Once you have a clearer picture, it's time to summarise this with a joint understanding of the facts and implications. This is about taking responsibility, being transparent about what you jointly know, and getting an agreement on this.

This is also the time to think about and explain what you have learned and what you will do differently next time. If you need time to do this and return to the client, then be clear that you intend to do that.

We all need to move forward without issues hanging over our heads. The summary must start at the beginning of your relationship so that it's not just about the problem but your ongoing relationship. This is a perfect time to summarise what has been achieved, the good points of your relationship, and the apparent issues.

**Summarise the problem**, what you shared, and what you learned from today's conversation. Explain what you have done so far to remedy the situation.

**Ask what the client wants to do now.**

> *"Given our discussion, what would you like to do now?"*

> *"What do you think is a fair way for us to move forward?"*

Remember, this is a discussion in a mature relationship, and the outcome should be acceptable to both parties. If the conversation is not moving that way, then agree on the points you can agree on and list the points of disagreement. Make a summary of what each party is going to do next.

Sometimes, this takes more than one meeting. If so, you must stay in charge by setting up the next actions and meetings.

**Reset the relationship.**

Agree on how you are going to move forward. Typically, there are three outcomes.

1. **They leave** – make it as easy as possible for them and work to help them to leave gracefully.
2. **They stay** – but there are still issues to solve. Work through a clear timetable and tasks and responsibilities. Follow this up in writing. Keep working until all issues are resolved.
3. **They stay** – and the issue is resolved. This is a great time to create and agree on new standards or rules for how you will work together. Follow this up in writing to show this has been actioned.

## Review – Repeat – Renew.

We need to continue connections, even when there aren't issues. Does this sound familiar? We get a new client (hooray), and then, from a sales perspective, we set and forget.

Always make a time (quarterly, bi-annually or annually) to catch up with your client to reaffirm your value, discuss discoveries and learn more about what may have changed for them. Ideally, your client will know about this from your Sales Roadmap (see Chapter 7).

The end of the project is another excellent time to talk to clients and understand from their perspective what went well and what you can learn and improve on.

A Review covers four main areas:

**Sales process.**

- What did they like about the sales process?
- Did you deliver to the expectations that were set in the sales process?
- Are there any suggestions for improvements in the sales process?

**Delivery process.**

- What did they like about the delivery process?
- Did you deliver to the expectations that were set during the delivery process?
- Are there any suggestions for improvements in the delivery process?

**The project / or work done.**

- What were your expected outcomes of this project?
- Did we meet these?
- Can you share any unexpected outcomes (positive and negative) from this project?
- Can we use this project as a case study on our website?
- Would you be prepared to write us a recommendation on your thoughts on working with us?

**The future.**

- You will often uncover other projects that could add value to the client through the delivery.
- Present those with a summary of what you uncovered and what a value-adding project might look like to improve this for them.
- Are there any future projects the client has in their timetable that you could work on or bid for?
- Are there any other associates in the same business or other businesses that you think we should be talking to?
  - Would you introduce us?
  - Can I use your name when I contact them?

## Sales Is Circular.

Selling and delivering to our clients doesn't stop. Partly, this is because we learn more about our clients as we work with them, and partly because things in business and life change.

To take advantage of this circle, you must connect with your clients repeatedly and ask them to dance. Introduce them to a new dance you have discovered, or check in to ensure they are still okay with the dance you started.

Practising our dance with the same client brings a rhythm and a level of comfort, understanding and trust. All these things allow us to gain greater insights into our clients and, perhaps more importantly, our impact on their business.

This is why we started our business in the first place – to make a difference. Reconnecting, remembering and adding to these stories fills our cup and makes up a vital part of the sales tools we can use to explain what we do and our impact on new clients.

Ultimately, **Great Selling** isn't about me winning over a client. **Great Selling** creates wonderful memories, new stories and discoveries that keep our wheels turning. **Great Selling** happens when we positively impact ourselves, our teams, our clients and the community. This Yellow Brick Road of value is what I want you to explore, understand and take people on.

But most of all, I want you to keep selling and the sales process going. You know it feeds you, and you love the connections and the learnings.

Enjoy your journey.

# Conclusion

> "Always remember you are braver than you believe, stronger than you seem and smarter than you think."
> — A.A. MILNE (MILNE, 1926)[19]

## Braver:

Thank you for walking with me through this book. You are braver and better at selling than you know. When I am working with people, they often say things like ... *'you make this look so easy."* My response – because it is.

Once you get out there and start sharing, listening and creating with your clients, you will see that you can do this. It isn't about not having fear. It's about knowing you are kind, genuine, and have something to offer. You must take the time to discover and find people who value that.

Bravery, like your attitude to selling, starts in your mind. Conquer that first.

## Stronger:

Strength doesn't come from trickery or muscles. It comes from perseverance and honesty. It takes more strength to say no to a "toxic client" or confront a problem that you've created than it does to walk boldly down the street, assuming that you are ten feet tall and bulletproof.

Selling is a muscle. You will get stronger the more you use it. Practise and find the right things that work for you and your client. Learn, document and share what works well in your situation. This will help demystify selling for others in your business.

Strength comes from activity. So go and be sales active and build your skills and muscles.

## Smarter:

Being smart isn't about having all the answers. A smart person can apply their knowledge to the situation before them. It's the listening, the timing and the application of the ideas and thoughts that make them smart.

Curiosity is the most essential thing in being smart. There is no point in being super-smart or great at what you do and not being able to share it. When you are curious, you listen and learn. This allows you to apply those smarts to **this** person and **this** situation.

Results in selling come from walking **with** people and showing how smart you are at helping them walk down the Yellow Brick Road. It's now about the destination; each step is a result and a chance to get smarter and learn more.

> "Everything has to come to an end, sometime."
> — L. FRANK BAUM, *THE MARVELOUS LAND OF OZ*

# Acknowledgements

There are so many people to say thank you to for this, my first book of many.

My Dad, who always taught us that we could do and be anything that we wanted. He always believed in me, even when and especially when I didn't. My Mum, who taught me grace and wisdom. She is always there to read and critique my writing.

To the countless mentors and mentees that I have had over my journey. Chris Pearson, for first schooling me in sales strategy and psychology. Thank you to Peter Hannan and Hannah Browne who both, in different ways encouraged me to be more.

To my clients over the years that always gave me lessons in selling, about what worked and what didn't. Without this witness, this experience, this book wouldn't exist. You all showed me what Great Selling really was, all I had to do was write it down and share it.

You will no doubt recognise from this book how much I love old movies and books. I particularly want to thank Frank L. Baum for his magnificent writings on Oz, amazing and beautiful. These stories allow us to explore our own frailty and journey in life. There is still so much to learn. I would also like to thank the courage of MGM in delivering The Wizard of Oz to us. This was an amazing movie in so many ways that I explore some of in this book.

To my kids, bonus kids and husband who were there for the whole journey with me, cheering me on.

Thank you to the professors at Melbourne Business School. They taught me perseverance, to be myself and to challenge and think. Especially Amanda Sinclair, Ian Harper, Mark Ritson and David Austin.

My wondrous and magical book coach, Anna Von Zinner. Her process has helped me easily birth this book after many years of failed attempts and false labours.

To the Alpha and Omega, who has known and encouraged me from the time in my mother's womb.

# About the Author

Frances is a mum, business owner and writer. She lives in Melbourne, Australia with her family. She has a young family and bonus kids so she knows what it is to juggle personal and business priorities. She knows that she isn't always successful – but she is always open and curious to trying new ideas that might make a positive difference.

She has a secret – she LOVES selling! But she knows, that to many, "sales" is a dirty word. She is on a mission to change that. Sales is the lifeblood of business and built on valuable relationships between you and your clients.

She is on a mission to demystify the sales process so that anyone can improve their sales activities and results, in a way that they love. Her vision is a world where business owners deeply understand and respect their clients and the art of sales.

She has had a career in sales as a top performing sales person, sales leader, business growth strategist and entrepreneur. For the last 13 years she has been helping businesses and women founders learn how to confidently connect with and convert their most loved clients.

Before getting married and having a family and whilst working full-time, she studied Change Management and completed an MBA from Melbourne Business School. Coupled with her hands on sales and business experience, this has created a toolbox of techniques and ideas to help businesses better understand themselves and their clients.

### Connect With Frances!

**LinkedIn:** https://www.linkedin.com/in/franpratt/

**Accelerate Sales** is her signature Sales Program to help women get better at selling: https://acceleratesales.online/

**Website:** www.metisan.com.au

# References

1. Source: Australian Small Business and Family Business Ombudsman. "Small Business Matters" June 2023. Link accessed 31/7/24 https://www.asbfeo.gov.au/sites/default/files/2023-06/Small%20Business%20Matters_June%202023.pdf
2. Maister, D.H., Green, C.H. & Galford, R.M. (2002). *The Trusted Advisor*. Simon & Schuster (US).
3. https://www.forbes.com/sites/blakemorgan/2019/04/29/does-it-still-cost-5x-more-to-create-a-new-customer-than-retain-an-old-one/?sh=260a840f3516, accessed 8/2/24.
4. Pink, D.H. (2013). *To Sell Is Human: The Surprising Truth About Moving Others*. Riverhead Books. Reprint edition.
5. Richter, S. (2009). *Take the Cold Out of Cold Calling*. Beaver's Pond Press.
6. https://www.jillkonrath.com/sales-blog/bid/107858/How-to-Really-Use-LinkedIn-to-Increase-Your-Sales Accessed 09/08/2024
7. This comes from the final speech in "The Great Dictator" movie: Source: accessed 31/7/2024 https://www.charliechaplin.com/en/films/7-The-Great-Dictator/articles/29-The-Final-Speech-from-The-Great-Dictator
8. Mehrabian, A. (1971). *Silent messages*. Wadsworth Publishing Company.
9. Lindahl, K. (2002). *The Sacred Art of Listening: Forty Reflections for Cultivating a Spiritual Practice*. Skylight Paths Pub.
10. Covey, S. R. (1989). *The 7 habits of highly effective people: Restoring the character ethic*. Free Press.
11. Cialdini, R. B. (2021). *Influence: The psychology of persuasion* (New and expanded ed.). Harper Business.

12. https://hbr.org/2012/05/to-get-better-decisions-get-a?cm_mmc=email-_-newsletter-_-management_tip-_-tip100912 (accessed 19/06/2023)
13. Schwartz, B. (2014). *The Paradox of Choice: Why More is Less*. Brilliance Audio (AudioBook)
14. Wise, R. (Director). (1965). *The Sound of Music* [Film]. 20th Century Fox.
15. https://www.liveabout.com/get-ready-to-sell-by-building-self-confidence-2947285 (accessed 5 July 2023)
16. Brooks, A. W. (2013). Get excited: Reappraising pre-performance anxiety as excitement improves performance. *Journal of Experimental Psychology: General, 143(3), 1144-1158. https://doi.org/10.1037/a0035325
17. Mehrabian, A. (1971). *Silent messages*. Wadsworth Publishing Company.
18. Brown, B. (2012). *Daring greatly: How the courage to be vulnerable transforms the way we live, love, parent, and lead*. Gotham Books.
19. Milne, A. A. (1926). *Winnie-the-Pooh*. E. P. Dutton.

www.ingramcontent.com/pod-product-compliance
Lightning Source LLC
Chambersburg PA
CBHW072150070526
44585CB00015B/1069